TABLE OF CONTENTS

Executive Summary

U.S. opyright laws have protected computer software for many years, and today that regime of legal protection supports an industry that is a major engine of economic growth. In the last quarter century, the software industry has added millions of jobs and increased the U.S. gross domestic product by hundreds of billions of dollars. Software has transformed our way of life, paving the way for personal computers, video games, digital photography, the internet, music and movie streaming services, smartphones, the Internet of Things, cryptocurrencies, and self-driving cars. In the near future, software will be behind even more innovations, like artificial intelligence and advanced robotics. In short, as one software entrepreneur famously put it, "software is eating the world."[1]

One result of the spread of software is that consumers now routinely use software-enabled products for everything from adjusting the thermostats in their homes, to driving to work, to getting a midnight snack from the fridge. This near-ubiquity has led some to question whether current copyright laws provide adequate guidance regarding the sometimes complex copyright issues arising in relation to software embedded in consumer products. These concerns span a wide range of uses, including resale, repair, research, and beyond. For example, to the extent that repairing a software-enabled device requires copying or altering a copyrighted computer program, does the law limit consumers' right to engage in such activity? How might consumers' ability to sell or convey such a device be affected if the embedded software is subject to a licensing agreement?

In light of these and other concerns, in October 2015, Chairman Chuck Grassley and Ranking Member Patrick Leahy of the Senate Judiciary Committee (the "Committee") requested that the Copyright Office provide its expert advice, in "an effort to better understand and evaluate how our copyright laws enable creative expression, foster innovative business models, and allow legitimate uses in this software-enabled environment."[2] Among other issues, the Committee requested that the Office study and report on: (1) the provisions of the copyright law that are implicated by the ubiquity of copyrighted software in everyday products; (2) the law's effect on the design, distribution, and legitimate uses of such products, as well as on innovative services related thereto; (3) the effects that statutory changes in this area could have on stakeholder interests and business models; and (4) the intersection of copyright provisions with other areas of law in this context.[3] The Committee also asked the Office

---

[1] Marc Andreessen, *Why Software Is Eating The World*, WALL ST. J. (Aug. 20, 2011), http://www.wsj.com/articles/SB10001424053111903480904576512250915629460.

[2] Letter from Chairman Chuck Grassley and Ranking Member Patrick Leahy, S. Comm. on the Judiciary, to Maria A. Pallante, Register of Copyrights & Dir., U.S. Copyright Office, at 1 (Oct. 22, 2015) ("Grassley/Leahy Letter"), http://www.copyright.gov/policy/software/grassley_leahy-software-study-request-10222015.pdf.

[3] *Id.* at 1-2.

to make appropriate legislative or other recommendations, if it believed changes were necessary.

The Committee's request was limited to embedded software in everyday products. The Committee did *not* ask the Office to review copyright law as applied to software and computer programs generally. Accordingly, a foundational issue in this Report is how to define the specific subset of software that is the subject of this study. As discussed in Part II, the Office found a general consensus that it would be a mistake to statutorily distinguish between software in everyday products and other kinds of software. At the same time, there is no question that the spread of software in everyday products raises unique issues. These products share certain common characteristics, and since the Office's focus is on products with these shared traits, the Office does not analyze software generally.

The Copyright Office endeavored to examine how existing copyright law doctrines might address the particular issues that arise with respect to these products. In Part III, the Report describes the relevant copyright law doctrines potentially operating in the context of software-enabled consumer products. In addition, the Report briefly identifies some of the complex issues outside of copyright—including privacy and cybersecurity—that have arisen in this context. These issues are being investigated by a number of other components of the federal government, including the Federal Trade Commission, the Department of Homeland Security, and the Department of Commerce. The Copyright Office's analysis is thus limited to the *copyright* issues presented by the spread of software-enabled consumer products.

Part IV then addresses how software-enabled consumer products can be resold, repaired or improved, researched for security flaws, or made to interoperate with other products or software. In each case, the Office finds that faithful application of existing copyright law doctrines should provide no barrier to legitimate uses. In short:

- The Office's study did not reveal evidence that consumers have been prevented from reselling or otherwise disposing of their software-enabled consumer products. The Office does not see a current need for legislative change relating to resale, so long as courts properly apply the first-sale right embodied in section 109 of the Copyright Act.

- The Office recognizes the value of allowing the public to freely repair defective consumer products and tinker with products to improve their function. But establishing a new statutory framework explicitly permitting repair and tinkering does not appear to be necessary at this time. Properly understood, existing copyright law doctrines—including the idea/expression dichotomy, fair use, merger, *scènes à faire*, and section 117—should continue to facilitate these types of activities.

- Similarly, the Office recognizes the value of allowing the public to engage in good-faith security research of software-enabled consumer products. Again, however, statutory changes (at least outside the context of the anticircumvention provisions in section 1201) do not appear to be necessary at present. Existing copyright law doctrines should protect this legitimate activity.

- The Office recognizes the significance of preserving the ability to develop products and services that can interoperate with software-enabled consumer products, and the related goal of preserving competition in the marketplace. While a new statutory framework might help reduce some uncertainty in this area, such action does not appear to be necessary at this time. Again, faithful application of existing copyright law doctrines can preserve the twin principles of interoperability and competition.

The Copyright Office also examined the reach and scope of licensing practices for embedded software, an issue that implicates several subsidiary issues, including: the relationship of the Copyright Act to state contract law; whether, and in what circumstances, violations of the terms of software licenses would constitute copyright infringement; and confusion among consumers regarding licensing terms for embedded software. The Office's study found that, in certain circumstances, such as resale, there is only limited evidence regarding real-world restrictions. Accordingly, the Office believes that the question of ownership versus licensing, while very important, is one that can be resolved with the proper application of existing case law.

The Copyright Office acknowledges that relying on flexible doctrines like merger, *scènes à faire*, and fair use brings less certainty than bright-line legislative fixes would; in some cases, clarification may only come after litigation. But formal application of copyright law to software-enabled consumer products is still relatively recent. In the context of the technologically driven products at issue in this Report, legislation carries its own risks, including that it might address the technologies of today but may fail to anticipate the different technologies—and distinct concerns—of tomorrow. In that respect, established copyright doctrines benefit from the ability to adapt more deftly to specific situations. As this Report demonstrates, copyright doctrines such as fair use, merger, and *scènes à faire* have regularly been extended and applied to new technologies as they have developed. And the Office offers this Report as a roadmap of sorts for those seeking to make legitimate use of embedded software.

In sum, the Copyright Office believes that existing copyright law is, at least at this time, well-suited to handle this new age of embedded software, so that innovators can continue to improve our lives and revolutionize our world.

I.   Background and Study History[4]

A.   Legal Background

When Congress passed the first federal copyright law in 1790, it protected only books, maps, and charts.[5] As time and technology marched on, however, Congress expanded protection to additional categories of works, from photographs to film, to sound recordings, and eventually, computer programs.[6] The earliest attempts to protect computer programs in the 1960s were somewhat inelegant, with the Copyright Office registering the first computer programs as "books" under the "Rule of Doubt."[7]

The United States has traveled far from the time of that first registration, to an age in which computer programs and software are major drivers of the economy and the distribution of information. Indeed, in the last quarter century, the software industry has added millions of jobs and increased the value of the U.S. gross domestic product ("GDP") by hundreds of billions of dollars.[8] The industry attributes much of this growth directly to copyright law.[9]

---

[4] All references to written comments submitted by participants in the Copyright Office's study are by party name (abbreviated where appropriate), followed by "Initial Comments" or "Reply Comments" (*e.g.*, "iFixit Initial Comments," "Copyright Alliance Reply Comments"). References to the transcripts of the Office's two hearings are by page and line number, date, and name and affiliation of speaker (*e.g.*, Tr. at 8:21-24 (May 24, 2016) (Sy Damle, U.S. Copyright Office)). Both written comments and transcripts of the roundtable hearings are available on the study website at http://www.copyright.gov/policy/software/.

[5] Act of May 31, 1790, ch. 15, § 1, 1 Stat. 124, 124.

[6] 17 U.S.C. §§ 101, 102(a), 106; U.S. COPYRIGHT OFFICE, COMPENDIUM OF U.S. COPYRIGHT OFFICE PRACTICES §§ 102.7, 503.1(B) (3d ed. 2014) ("COMPENDIUM (THIRD)").

[7] The first Office registration was for two computer programs—one on magnetic tape and the other printed on paper—as "books." *See Computer Program Copyrighted for First Time*, N.Y. TIMES 43, May 8, 1964, at 43, 51; *see also* U.S. COPYRIGHT OFFICE, CIRCULAR 31D (1965). For more information on the "Rule of Doubt," *see* COMPENDIUM (THIRD) § 607.

[8] BUS. SOFTWARE ALL., THE $1 TRILLION ECONOMIC IMPACT OF SOFTWARE 3 (2016), http://softwareimpact.bsa.org/pdf/Economic_Impact_of_Software_Report.pdf (finding that, in 2014, the software industry added $475.3 billion dollars to the GDP and employed 2.5 million people); ROBERT J. SHAPIRO, SOFTWARE & INFO. INDUS. ASS'N, THE U.S. SOFTWARE INDUSTRY: AN ENGINE FOR ECONOMIC GROWTH AND EMPLOYMENT 2 (2014), https://www.siia.net/Admin/FileManagement.aspx/LinkClick.aspx?fileticket=yLPW0SrBfk4%3D&portalid=0 (noting that between 1997 and 2012, software industry production increased from $149 billion to $425 billion, and that direct employment in the software industry also increased from 778,000 jobs in 1990 to 2.5 million jobs in 2014).

[9] *See* BSA Initial Comments at 2-3 ("The existing U.S. copyright framework for software has given rise to the most innovative and diverse software industry in the world," and "we are on the cusp of an era of even greater software-driven innovation, due in large measure to strong and comprehensive copyright protection for software."); Copyright Alliance Initial Comments at 2 (noting that "copyright drives innovation in the software industry, an industry that is flourishing in the digital age under the current legal framework"); ESA Initial Comments at 2 (asserting that "strong copyright protection for software (embedded and

Today, the law is well-settled that computer programs generally are protected by copyright law, and are governed by the same doctrines as other types of works. In the Copyright Act of 1976, Congress acknowledged that copyright law covers computer programs, while simultaneously removing from protection "any idea, procedure, process, system, method of operation, concept, principle, or discovery, regardless of the form in which it is described, explained, illustrated, or embodied in such work."[10] Congress also created the National Commission on New Technological Uses of Copyrighted Works ("CONTU") to study issues raised by new technologies, including computers.[11] Congress eventually followed CONTU's recommendations to define "computer programs" in the Act and to amend section 117 to allow copies or adaptations of computer programs to be made either "as an essential step" of using the computer, or for archival purposes.[12]

Over subsequent years, Congress has addressed computer programs periodically by, among other things, passing the Computer Software Rental Amendments Act of 1990 ("CSRAA"),[13] which created a narrow exception to the first-sale doctrine by prohibiting the rental, lease, or lending of computer programs, and by amending section 117 yet again in the Digital Millennium Copyright Act ("DMCA") to preserve independent repair.[14] Throughout this period, Congress has continually maintained a robust copyright regime for software.

Though the scope of copyright protection for software has been relatively stable over time, the marketplace is changing; some would say radically. The reach of software is almost infinite. In the past, "consumer software was typically found in standalone applications and operating systems that ran primarily on desktop or laptop computers."[15] It could also be found in "[l]imited categories of software-enabled consumer products . . ., including early video game consoles, calculators, and microwaves, but these were the exception rather than the rule."[16] By contrast, "[t]oday's

---

otherwise) has been a tremendous policy success that has enabled decades of innovation and creativity in product design and functionality"); Microsoft Initial Comments at 5 (stating that "software developers have relied on copyright protection for over four decades to justify massive investments in software innovation"); SIIA Initial Comments at 5 (stating that the "market ecosystem [for software] has spawned frenetically paced innovation and development while maintaining the incentives to create that the copyright law provides").

[10] 17 U.S.C. § 102(b).

[11] Pub. L. No. 93-573, § 201, 88 Stat. 1873, 1873-74 (1974); *see also* CONTU, FINAL REPORT 9 (1978) ("CONTU Report").

[12] *See* CONTU Report at 12-13; Act of Dec. 12, 1980, Pub. L. No. 96-517, § 10, 94 Stat. 3015, 3028-29.

[13] Pub. L. No. 101-650, tit.8, 104 Stat. 5089, 5134-37 (1990) (codified at 17 U.S.C. § 109(b)).

[14] 144 CONG. REC. S11,890 (daily ed. Oct. 8, 1998) (statement of Sen. Leahy).

[15] Engine Advocacy Initial Comments at 1.

[16] *Id.*

consumer products and devices—from smartphones and home appliances to vehicles and medical devices—integrate software code. That code doesn't just offer new bells and whistles that improve on existing products; it is essential to the basic functionality of many devices."[17] Software is now nearly ubiquitous and, "[a]s parts increasingly incorporate computer software, functions that used to be performed by hardware components now are controlled by software embedded in those parts."[18] The incorporation of networking capabilities into consumer products has led to the "Internet of Things."[19] Indeed, "we are in the midst of a transformational new generation of software innovation. Smartphones, tablets, and other mobile devices not only provide computing 'on the go,' they also are bringing billions of new users online."[20]

This boom in technology embedded in everyday products is not altogether unanticipated. Including software in "consumer devices is hardly a new phenomenon; a huge number of 'everyday products,' including microwave ovens and handheld calculators, have since the early-1970s featured embedded software."[21] As noted, copyright law has been credited by some as paving the way for these new technological advances,[22] and the public has benefited greatly from the new and creative ways that everyday products enhance their lives, and will continue to benefit from the possibility of further innovation.[23]

Nevertheless, the spread of software in recent years has led some to question whether the current state of copyright law is sufficient to handle the sometimes complex

---

[17] Aaron Perzanowski et al. Initial Comments at 1.

[18] Auto Care Ass'n Initial Comments at 3 (noting also that "[t]oday's engines, transmissions, oxygen sensors, ignitions, brakes, emissions systems, electric windows, air blowers, air bags, and even windshield wipers are just a few of the systems in which manufacturers have replaced purely electro-mechanical parts with microprocessors and software controls. The function of these parts is the same regardless of whether implemented in hardware or software.").

[19] *See* Afua Bruce, Dan Correa & Suhas Subramanyam, *Internet of Things: Examining Opportunities and Challenges*, WHITE HOUSE: BLOG (Aug. 30, 2016), https://www.whitehouse.gov/blog/2016/08/30/internet-things-examining-opportunities-and-challenges.

[20] Microsoft Initial Comments at 2.

[21] BSA Initial Comments at 1; *see also* ESA Initial Comments at 3-4.

[22] Copyright Alliance Initial Comments at 13 ("Copyright plays a significant role in this innovation boom. It is a critical driver of technological innovation and economic competitiveness."); ESA Initial Comments at 7 ("Copyright law is largely responsible for providing necessary incentives for both game and game device makers – ensuring they have the ability to expand features and access and still protect their innovation.").

[23] BSA Initial Comments at 3 ("Consumers now have access to a range of IoT [Internet of Things] products capable of improving 'conservation, efficiency, productivity, public safety, health, education and more.'" (citation omitted)); CCIA Initial Comments at 1 ("As the Office's notice observes, the omnipresence of software in modern consumer products has greatly improved features and functions for users."); Engine Advocacy Initial Comments at 1 ("The increasing prevalence of software-enabled products and the rise of the Internet of Things offers great value to consumers, businesses, and other users of the vast array of innovative products in which such software will be found.").

copyright issues that arise. While copyright infringement is always a concern,[24] there also have been challenges relating to how consumers access their devices, and questions regarding how existing law can be applied fairly to this specific subset of everyday products. For example, some have expressed concern over the impact of embedded software on consumers' expectation of ownership of their personal property. Noting that the embedded software in a number of devices is licensed, rather than sold, to the device purchaser, they have argued that the current law allows manufacturers to exercise undue control over secondary markets by restricting transfers of the software to third parties.[25] Others have argued that the law does not adequately address the need of many parties to copy or modify embedded software for legitimate purposes, such as repair, security research, or the development of interoperable products.[26]

Members of Congress have introduced legislation to respond to some of these challenges. To address issues surrounding licensing of embedded software, in 2014 and again in 2015, Representatives Blake Farenthold and Jared Polis introduced the You Own Devices Act ("YODA"), which would extend the first-sale doctrine to allow the owner of a "machine or other product" that uses a computer program to transfer a copy of the computer program when the machine or other product is sold, leased, or otherwise transferred to another person.[27] The right to transfer would not be waivable by contract.[28] Additionally, in 2013 and 2015, Representative Zoe Lofgren introduced the Unlocking Technology Act, which addresses the copyright implications of copying or

---

[24] *See, e.g.,* ESA Initial Comments at 10 ("[I]n the absence of strong copyright protection for software, potential competitors can and will discern and copy embedded software, because that is an easier path to getting to market with a software-enabled product than creating original software. As a result, copyright infringement is a concern for embedded software as well as for software intended to be used on a general-purpose computer.") (citation omitted); ACT Initial Comments at 2 ("Piracy presents a major threat to the success of ACT members and the billions of consumers who rely on digital products and services.").

[25] *See First Sale Under Title 17: Hearing Before the Subcomm. on Courts, Intell. Prop., and the Internet of the H. Comm. on the Judiciary,* 113th Cong. 47 (2014) (testimony of Jonathan Band, Owners' Rights Initiative) ("[By] interfering with resale, . . . license terms harm both the consumers who want to sell the products and the secondary consumers, often government agencies, that want to buy them.").

[26] *See, e.g.,* Perzanowski et al. Initial Comments at 5-6 ("[The law] give[s] rights holders the power to control whether and how consumers use the devices they own; when and under what conditions they can lend, resell, or give them away; who can repair them; what interoperable products, replacement parts, and components can be used with them; the degree to which those products can be researched and tested; the possibility of tinkering and user innovation; and the availability of interoperable products." (citation omitted)); Engine Advocacy Initial Comments at 9-10 ("As licensees of the copyrighted software in their products, consumers may be lawfully unable to copy, modify, and resell the software in their devices," particularly in order "to tinker with, improve, repair and/or sell devices and other property they have purchased."); Public Knowledge/OTI Initial Comments at 11 ("Copyright law can, at times, frustrate consumer expectations about product interoperability and make it impossible for third parties to produce interoperable products.").

[27] *See* H.R. 862, 114th Cong.§ 2(a) (2015); H.R. 5586, 113th Cong. § 2(a) (2014).

[28] H.R. 862, 114th Cong. § 2(a) (2015); H.R. 5586, 113th Cong. § 2(a) (2014).

adapting the software of mobile communications devices to connect to wireless networks.[29] It would amend section 117 to allow such copying or adapting if initiated by or with the consent of the owner of the device, and if the owner is in legal possession of that device and has permission to connect to the wireless network.[30]

B.   *Study History*

In October 2015, Chairman Chuck Grassley and Ranking Member Patrick Leahy of the Senate Judiciary Committee requested that the Copyright Office provide expert input on software-embedded consumer products. The request noted that "[a]s software plays an ever-increasing role in defining consumer interactions with devices and products, many questions are being asked about how consumers can lawfully use products that rely on software to function."[31] The letter explained that the request was "an effort to better understand and evaluate how our copyright laws enable creative expression, foster innovative business models, and allow legitimate uses in this software-enabled environment."[32] The request specifically asked that the Office study and report on the following:

- The provisions of the copyright law that are implicated by the ubiquity of copyrighted software in everyday products;

- Whether, and to what extent, the design, distribution, and legitimate uses of products are being enabled and/or frustrated by the application of existing copyright law to software in everyday products;

- Whether, and to what extent, innovative services are being enabled and/or frustrated by the application of existing copyright law to software in everyday products;

- Whether, and to what extent, legitimate interests or business models for copyright owners and users could be undermined or improved by changes to the copyright law in this area; and

---

[29] H.R. 1892, 113th Cong. § 3 (2013); H.R. 1587, 114th Cong. § 3 (2015). If passed, this legislation would also amend 17 U.S.C. § 1201(a) to allow for circumvention of technological measures if the purpose of such circumvention was to engage in a use that does not infringe copyright. H.R. 1892, 113th Cong. § 2 (2013); H.R. 1587, 114th Cong. § 2 (2015)

[30] H.R. 1892, 113th Cong. § 3 (2013); H.R. 1587, 114th Cong. § 3 (2015).

[31] Grassley/Leahy Letter at 1.

[32] *Id.*

- The key issues in how copyright law intersects with other areas of law in establishing how products that rely on software to function can be lawfully used.[33]

The Committee also asked the Office whether legislative changes are necessary. This request was limited to embedded software in everyday products, which, as described in detail below, is a category rather resistant to clear definitions. The Committee did *not* ask the Office to look into copyright law as applied to software and computer programs generally.[34]

Over the course of a little more than a year, the Copyright Office studied the Committee's questions by soliciting public comments and holding roundtable hearings on both coasts. The Office began this process by publishing a Notice of Inquiry in the Federal Register in December 2015,[35] which requested public comment on the five topics listed in the Committee's letter. The Notice of Inquiry also suggested that, when responding to the Committee's questions, commenters also consider the following points:

- Whether copyright law should distinguish between software embedded in "everyday products" and other types of software, and, if so, how such a distinction might be drawn in an administrable manner.

---

[33] *Id.* at 2.

[34] A number of commenters also noted the interrelationship between the issues studied here and those raised by the anti-circumvention provisions in section 1201. *See, e.g.*, R Street Institute Initial Comments at 1. The issues raised by section 1201, however, are at once broader and narrower than the issues raised by this study. They are broader, in part, because section 1201 applies to *all* copyrighted works, not just software, and thus raises additional issues that are beyond the scope of this study. At the same time, section 1201 deals with a narrower range of legal issues: it has no relevance to the scope of consumer rights in products that do not have technological protection measures attached to them, or to issues like resale that do not require circumvention of such measures. Accordingly, the Office is studying issues related to section 1201 as part of a separate and concurrent study. For more information on that study, *see* http://copyright.gov/policy/1201/.

In addition, The Committee did not ask for the Office's views on issues involving the registration of computer programs, and none of the participants raised this issue in their comments or at the roundtables. That said, the Office has initiated an academic partnership with Professor Paul Goldstein, Professor Luciana Herman, and students at Stanford Law School to gather information from relevant stakeholders on software registration issues. The Stanford team will use this information to develop recommendations for the Office, which can potentially be used in preparing a formal notice of inquiry or notice of proposed rulemaking. *See Copyright Policy Practicum: Revising the Requirements for Computer Software Registration*, STANFORD LAW SCHOOL LAW & POLICY LAB, https://law.stanford.edu/education/only-at-sls/law-policy-lab/practicums-2016-2017/copyright-policy-practicum-revising-the-requirements-for-computer-software-registration/.

[35] Software-Enabled Consumer Products Study: Notice and Request for Public Comment, 80 Fed. Reg. 77,668 (Dec. 15, 2015) ("2015 Notice of Inquiry"). This Notice of Inquiry and the Office's additional Federal Register Notice are attached as Appendix A.

- ○ Whether "everyday products" can be distinguished from other products that contain software, such as general purpose computers—essentially how to define "everyday products."

- ○ If distinguishing between software embedded in "everyday products" and other types of software is impracticable, whether there are alternative ways the Office can distinguish between categories of software.

- The rationale for and proper scope of copyright protection for software embedded in everyday products, including the extent to which copyright infringement is a concern with respect to such software.

- The need to enable interoperability with software-embedded devices, including specific examples of ways in which the law frustrates or enables such interoperability.

- Whether current limitations on and exceptions to copyright protection adequately address issues concerning software embedded in everyday products, or whether amendments or clarifications would be useful. Specific areas of interest include:

  - ○ The idea/expression dichotomy (codified in 17 U.S.C. § 102(b))

  - ○ The merger doctrine

  - ○ The *scènes à faire* doctrine

  - ○ Fair use (codified in 17 U.S.C. § 107)

  - ○ The first-sale doctrine (codified in 17 U.S.C. § 109)

  - ○ Statutory limitations on exclusive rights in computer programs (codified in 17 U.S.C. § 117)

- The state of contract law *vis-à-vis* software embedded in everyday products, and how contracts such as end user license agreements impact investment in and the dissemination and use of everyday products, including whether any legislative action in this area is needed.[36]

The Office received twenty-six initial written comments in response to its notice from a wide range of interested parties, including representatives from the software industry, legal scholars, and public interest groups.[37] The Office also received six reply comments

---

[36] *Id.* at 77,671-72.

[37] A list of participants in the study—both those who provided written comments and those who participated in roundtable hearings—is attached as Appendix B.

responding to issues raised by the initial written comments. In May 2016, the Office conducted public roundtables in Washington, D.C. and San Francisco, California.[38] During these roundtables, interested parties representing a variety of viewpoints discussed the topics identified in the Notice of Inquiry and other issues pertaining to software in consumer products, and whether the Copyright Act might be improved in this area.

During the study, the Office identified a number of notable issues. One foundational issue is how to define the specific subset of software that is the focus of the Committee's request. Most commenters declared that it would be nearly impossible to agree on an explicit definition of software embedded in everyday products,[39] and there was concern about how findings limited to a specific set of software could spill over, or not, into how copyright law applies to other types of software. Moreover, there was extensive discussion of copyright law and how it interacts with a consumer's ability to repair or resell an everyday product, or how researchers may conduct security testing. Interoperability and innovation were key concerns, with commenters on all sides weighing in on how copyright law interacts with embedded software in everyday devices. And, underlying much of this discussion was the reach and scope of licensing practices for software regarding these products, an issue that is intertwined with state law.

II.   Defining "Software Embedded in Everyday Products"

The Committee's letter reflected a basic—and correct—intuition that, as copyrighted software is embedded into a greater diversity of products, careful thought must be given to how copyright affects consumers' ability to engage in traditional uses of those products. These concerns are particularly acute with respect to products that have not required software to operate in the past. The Committee highlighted "our refrigerators, our cars, our farm equipment, [and] our wireless phones."[40] Other examples identified by commenters included kitchen appliances, thermostats, light bulbs, power tools, rice cookers, smoke alarms, dolls and toys, and similar types of consumer products.[41] At the same time, the Copyright Office understands that the Committee is *not* questioning the

---

[38] Software-Enabled Consumer Products Study and Section 1201 Study: Announcement of Public Roundtables, 81 Fed. Reg. 17,206 (Mar. 28, 2016).

[39] *But see* Public Knowledge/OTI Initial Comments at 1-2 (urging that the "distinction is not difficult to make" and distinguishing between "[a] consumer who buys software on magnetic, optical, or flash media" and one "who buys a laptop computer, tablet, car, health device, thermostat, or any other product that may contain software").

[40] Grassley/Leahy Letter at 1.

[41] Public Knowledge/OTI Initial Comments at 1, 2; Engine Advocacy Initial Comments at 1; Tr. at 25:21-26:02 (May 18, 2016) (Jonathan Bergmayer, Public Knowledge). ESA contended video game platforms should be excluded from this study, because they do not qualify as everyday devices. ESA Initial Comments at 1.

value of copyright protection of software in general. Thus, as the Notice of Inquiry stressed, the Office undertook "a highly specific study not intended to examine or address more general questions about software and copyright protection."[42]

The Office agrees with the Committee that copyright law's application to embedded software in certain kinds of products raises particular issues, including the relationship of copyright law in this context to resale, repair, tinkering, security research, and interoperability. The products affected by these concerns appear to share some common characteristics. To begin with, they are consumer-grade, rather than industrial devices, the latter of which may be subject to contractual and licensing agreements between parties with similar bargaining power. Further, the embedded software within the product often is specifically created for a particular product to control that product's basic operation. It may be that the embedded software is, at least to some degree, ancillary to the non-software (*e.g.,* mechanical or electrical) components of the product. The software may be distributed along with the product itself without payment of a separate charge or fee. It may be that the software is also not readily copied, thus presenting somewhat diminished concerns about widespread infringement.[43] The Office thus focused its study—and the analysis provided in this Report—on types of software that share these traits.[44]

---

[42] 2015 Notice of Inquiry at 77,668.

[43] Public Knowledge/OTI Initial Comments at 2; *cf.* 17 U.S.C. § 109(b)(1)(B)(i) (permitting rental of software-embedded products where the software cannot be copied during the ordinary operation or use of the device). This is not to say that infringement is not a concern in the context of embedded software. But the record suggests that such infringement may occur at the corporate, rather than the consumer, level. For instance, to the extent that embedded software is so creative that it gives a developer an advantage in the marketplace, other competitors may have an incentive to copy that software for use in their own products. Tr. at 36:15-37:06 (May 18, 2016) (Steve Tepp, GIPC); *see also* Tr. at 56:17-19 (May 18, 2016) (Jonathan Zuck, ACT) (stating that commoditization "can undermine investment in innovation" if it occurs too soon in the product development cycle); Tr. at 15:18-21 (May 24, 2016) (Evan Cox, BSA) ("People who have introduced products in th[e hoverboard] market have been swamped instantly by people who copy the software, take it apart, copy it, make it in China, re-import it [into the United States]."). BSA explained that, in such a situation, unauthorized copying by "low-cost competitors" poses a significant threat to software developers. Tr. at 15:01-06 (May 24, 2016) (Evan Cox, BSA). Concerns about commercial piracy, however, can be addressed on a case-by-case basis, applying existing doctrines of copyright law.

[44] The Copyright Office evaluated a number of other possible ways to distinguish these kinds of embedded software from software in general, but found them to be not particularly helpful. For example, the Office considered whether a distinction could be drawn between consumer products and commercial products. *See* Tr. at 24:01-09 (May 18, 2016) (Jonathan Bergmayer, Public Knowledge). Commenters, however, generally agreed that this differentiation would not be helpful, because consumer products can be used for commercial purposes (and *vice versa*). Tr. at 10:11-16 (May 18, 2016) (Jonathan Band, Owners' Rights Initiative) (stating that this is not "a helpful distinction"); Tr. at 29:19-22 (May 24, 2016) (Cathy Gellis, Digital Age Defense) (stating that "there's no real way of delineating which objects would get protection and which objects would get different sorts of protection or none whatsoever"). Another suggestion was to focus on the functional nature of some software as a potential differentiating tool for embedded software. Auto Care Ass'n Initial Comments at 8-9 (noting that a "bright line distinction [that] can be drawn for software that

The Copyright Office, however, was unable to distill the universe of embedded software into a simple legislative definition, which also precludes the Office from offering specific legislative text addressing this type of embedded software. The comments and roundtable testimony revealed a consensus that drawing a legislative distinction would be unworkable in practice.[45] Indeed, as several commenters observed, drawing such distinctions as a matter of copyright law is complicated by the evolving nature of the universe of these items. Any such attempt inevitably would be based on software-enabled devices currently existing in the marketplace, and based on Congress's understanding of the current state of the art. But technology is constantly changing, and new products likely will continue to enter the market at an increasingly rapid rate.[46] For example, today's consumer products such as wristwatches or smoke alarms "contain more computing power and more sophisticated software than personal computers did

---

controls the physical operation of a product"); Tr. at 28:07-09 (May 18, 2016) (Shaun Bockert, Dorman Products, Inc.) (distinguishing "software that serves a primarily functional role in a product"). In the Office's view, however, these distinctions would be impracticable. Relying on whether the software controls the *physical* operation of a product seems underinclusive, as it excludes many types of software that do not control mechanical processes but might nevertheless raise the kinds of concerns that motivated the Committee's letter. For instance, such a distinction could exclude software in "smart home" devices that simply communicate with and control other devices. Moreover, a test focused on the "functionality" of software is likely to be extremely overinclusive, since all software is functional to some degree. *See* 17 U.S.C. § 101 (defining "computer program" as "a set of statements or instructions to be used directly or indirectly in a computer in order to bring about a certain result").

[45] *See, e.g.,* BSA Initial Comments at 2 ("[T]he entire software industry is highly dynamic and interconnected, which makes it virtually impossible to draw any principled distinction between embedded and non-embedded software."); ACT Initial Comments at 5 (explaining that it "strongly discourages Congress and the USCO from attempting to distinguish between software embedded in 'everyday products' and other types of software . . . because such an exercise is impractical and would multiply confusion around the application of copyright law"); Aaron Perzanowski et al. Initial Comments at 12 ("[I]t would be unwise to distinguish software embedded in everyday products from software installed on traditional computers."); Microsoft Initial Comments at 9 (urging "the Copyright Office not to recommend changes to copyright protection for software embedded in consumer products"); Tr. at 9:22-23 (May 24, 2016) (Andrew Shore, Owners' Rights Initiative) ("[W]e shouldn't balkanize the code by drawing these distinctions."); Tr. at 23:01-04 (May 18, 2016) (Ben Golant, ESA) ("[T]here can't be any line drawing because that would be regulatory chaos to say this kind of software is not protected or this kind of software should be treated differently.").

[46] ACT Initial Comments at 5 ("[T]he exponential growth of the mobile app economy (and the 'Internet of Things' [IoT]) gives rise to a wider application of copyright law to many 'everyday' products."); CDT Initial Comments at 6 (attempting to distinguish everyday products "does not make much sense at the outset, and is changing every day owing to [the] pace of growth of the Internet of Things"); ESA Initial Comments at 2-3 (noting that "it would be unwise" to define everyday products, given "the pace of change").

20 years ago."[47] Thus, there is the very real concern that definitions based on an understanding of the current ecosystem would become quickly obsolete.[48]

Creating separate legislative categories for different types of products or software may also have unintended consequences.[49] If the law provides more expansive legal benefits for certain types of products or software, manufacturers may have an incentive to reengineer their products to fit within those definitions.[50] Conversely, if the law limits or eliminates legal benefits for other products or software, manufacturers may have an incentive to remove features benefiting consumers, or to add extraneous features that increase costs without providing corresponding benefits for the consumer.[51] Creating these types of distinctions may discourage manufacturers from developing enhancements that could improve the efficiency of their products.

Although the Copyright Office has concluded that copyright law should not formally differentiate between types of software and the products in which software may be found, copyright law's application to certain software does raise the particular issues mentioned above. In the following sections, the Report examines how existing copyright law doctrines might address these concerns. This Report, however, should be understood as focusing on embedded software sharing the common characteristics described above, rather than opining on software more generally. The Office is not suggesting a new test or rule to be applied by courts when analyzing or assessing software with these characteristics. Rather, the Office recognizes that certain doctrines such as fair use, merger, and *scènes à faire*, should be applied in a manner that is mindful of the overall context that is unique to this type of software.

---

[47] Public Knowledge/OTI Initial Comments at 2; BSA Initial Comments at 3; Tr. at 12:05-09 (May 18, 2016) (Christian Troncoso, BSA) ("10 years ago, we would never have imagined . . . that the phones in our pockets now have the computing power that . . . exceeds that which NASA used to land people on the moon in the '60s.").

[48] *See* ACT Initial Comments at 5 (cautioning that "technological innovation consistently outpaces legislative and regulatory processes, virtually assuring that any statutory articulation of a distinction will quickly become outdated, leading to more confusion and frustration in the marketplace").

[49] BSA Initial Comments at 2; Copyright Alliance Initial Comments at 3; ESA Initial Comments at 2-3; SIIA Initial Comments at 6.

[50] Public Knowledge/OTI Initial Comments at 2 ("Creating different legal rules for general-purpose computing platforms and single-purpose devices could create a perverse incentive for manufacturers or developers to conform their products to one category or the other."); Tr. at 19:12-14 (May 18, 2016) (Jonathan Zuck, ACT) (predicting that "you will change artificially the way that people implement their technology in order to find ways to get protection for what they're doing as opposed to actually creating more innovation").

[51] Copyright Alliance Reply Comments at 2 (noting that attempting to differentiate everyday products "could adversely affect incentives, investment, and innovation across many differ sectors of the economy—leading to numerous and substantial unintended consequences"); Public Knowledge/OTI Initial Comments at 2 ("Consumer demand, creative vision, and business considerations should factor into what new products come to market—not arcane copyright distinctions.").

III.   Relevant Legal Doctrines

As discussed above, the Committee asked the Copyright Office to discuss "the provisions of the copyright law that are implicated by the ubiquity of copyrighted software in everyday products."[52] In addition, the Committee requested that the Office "identify key issues in how copyright law intersects with other areas of law in establishing how products that rely on software to function can be lawfully used."[53]

A.   Basics of Copyright Protection

Although defining the universe of software-enabled everyday products may be somewhat fluid, the underlying principles of copyright law applying to the software in such products are well-established and well-known. As explained above, software generally has been protected by copyright law for decades, and is subject to a variety of familiar doctrines.

It is well-settled that computer code can be copyrightable as a "literary work."[54] The Copyright Act defines a "computer program" as "a set of statements or instructions to be used directly or indirectly in a computer in order to bring about a certain result."[55] Copyright protects both the "source code," which consists of words, numbers, and symbols typed by a programmer, as well as the compiled "object code," which is used by the computer to carry out the instructions, but generally cannot be read by a human being.[56]

To qualify for copyright protection, a computer program—like any other work of authorship—must be original. The Supreme Court has explained that the originality requirement is "not particularly stringent."[57] The work must be independently created by the author (not be copied from another work) and must possess "at least some minimal degree of creativity."[58] The vast majority of works satisfy this requirement easily because most "possess some creative spark, 'no matter how crude, humble or obvious' it might be."[59] But the fact that a computer program is original and therefore *eligible* for copyright protection under section 102(a) does not necessarily mean that every aspect of the program is protected. The copyright in a computer program—or any

---

[52] Grassley/Leahy Letter at 2.

[53] *Id.*

[54] 1-2A MELVILLE B. NIMMER AND DAVID NIMMER, NIMMER ON COPYRIGHT § 2A.10 (2015) ("NIMMER ON COPYRIGHT").

[55] 17 U.S.C. § 101.

[56] *See Apple Comput., Inc. v. Franklin Comput. Corp.*, 714 F.2d 1240, 1248-49 (3d Cir. 1983).

[57] *Feist Publ'ns v. Rural Tel. Serv. Co.*, 499 U.S. 340, 358 (1991).

[58] *Id.* at 345.

[59] *Id.* (citation omitted).

other work of authorship—protects only the original expression that the author contributed to that work.

The Copyright Act provides the owner of copyright in an original work of authorship, the "exclusive rights to do and to authorize" specified things with that work.[60] As most relevant here, these include the rights to (1) reproduce the work in copies, (2) prepare derivative works based on the original work, (3) distribute copies of the work to the public "by sale or other transfer of ownership, or by rental, lease, or lending," and (4) display the work publicly.[61] Those exclusive rights are the same for a computer program as they are for a book or a song; they are not diminished simply because the software code has some functional purpose.

B.   *Limits on the Scope of Copyright Protection*

The scope of the exclusive rights discussed above are subject to exceptions and limitations set forth in the Copyright Act and various judicial doctrines. In the specific factual circumstances where they apply, these doctrines serve to limit protection for software code, or even exclude it from protection entirely.

1.   Idea / Expression Dichotomy

Section 102(b) of the Copyright Act provides that "[i]n no case does copyright protection for an original work of authorship extend to any idea, procedure, process, system, method of operation, concept, principle, or discovery, regardless of the form in which it is described, explained, illustrated, or embodied in such work."[62] This provision codifies a long-standing principle of copyright law known as the idea/expression dichotomy.[63] "Taken literally, 'idea' refers to the work's animating concept—the idea, for example, of a drama about two star-crossed lovers—while 'expression' refers to the precise words in which the playwright wrote the drama."[64] Thus, properly read, section 102(b) draws a line between non-expressive intellectual concepts—whether considered ideas, principles, procedures, processes, etc.—which are *not* subject to copyright protection, and the expression that embodies them, which is.[65]

---

[60] *See* 17 U.S.C. § 106.

[61] *Id.*

[62] 17 U.S.C. § 102(b).

[63] *Golan v. Holder*, 565 U.S. 302, 328 (2012) ("The idea/expression dichotomy is codified at 17 U.S.C. § 102(b).").

[64] Paul Goldstein, Goldstein on Copyright § 2.3.1 (2015).

[65] 1-2 Nimmer on Copyright § 2.03[D][1] ("[A]lthough Section 102(b) denies that copyright may 'extend to' an 'idea, procedure, process,' as contained in a given work, it does not deny copyright to the work itself, merely because it consists of an 'idea, procedure, process,' etc.").

This interpretation of the statutory text is buttressed by the legislative history of the Act, which illustrates that the purpose of section 102(b) was to codify the dichotomy between abstract idea and concrete expression. The House Report on the 1976 Act, considered an authoritative source for the meaning of the Act,[66] stated expressly that "[s]ection 102(b) in no way enlarges or contracts the scope of copyright protection under the present law," but "[i]ts purpose is to restate, in the context of the new single Federal system of copyright, that the basic dichotomy between expression and idea remains unchanged."[67] Particularly notable is the House Report's discussion of the relevance of section 102(b) to the scope of protection for computer programs under the Act:

> Some concern has been expressed lest copyright in computer programs should extend protection to the methodology or processes adopted by the programmer, rather than merely to the "writing" expressing his ideas. Section 102(b) is intended, among other things, to make clear that the expression adopted by the programmer is the copyrightable element in a computer program, and that the actual processes or methods embodied in the program are not within the scope of the copyright law.[68]

Thus, the idea/expression dichotomy, as applied to software, excludes from copyright protection the abstract "methodology or processes adopted by the programmer" in creating the code.[69] It makes clear that the copyright law does not prevent anyone from studying the code for an existing program for the purpose of identifying the underlying ideas or processes embodied in that program. Nor does it prevent them from writing new routines or entirely new programs performing those same functions. They are free to use any of the ideas, methods, or other insights that make the program work—so long as they do not copy the specific lines of code from the existing program.

The applicability of section 102(b) in the context of embedded software is addressed in greater depth in Parts IV.B, C, and D, below.

2. Merger and *Scènes à Faire*

The merger doctrine—which is closely related to the idea/expression dichotomy—recognizes that there may be situations in which there is only one way or a limited number of ways to convey the idea that an author seeks to express.[70] In such a case, the author's expression may be inseparable from the idea embodied therein and cannot be protected by copyright law, because that would give the author a monopoly over the

---

[66] *See, e.g., Feist Publ'ns,* 499 U.S. at 355.

[67] H.R. REP. NO. 94-1476, at 57 *reprinted in* 1976 U.S.C.C.A.N. 5659, 5670.

[68] *Id.; see also* CONTU Report at 22 ("[C]opyright leads to the result that anyone is free to make a computer carry out any unpatented process, but not to misappropriate another's writing to do so.").

[69] H.R. REP. NO. 94-1476, at 57 *reprinted in* 1976 U.S.C.C.A.N. 5659, 5670.

[70] 1-2 NIMMER ON COPYRIGHT § 13.03[B][3].

idea itself, thereby preventing others from using that same idea in other works.[71] Conversely, "if a work's idea can be expressed in more than one way, courts will protect the copyright owner's expression even though the nature of the underlying idea closely circumscribes the variety of other possible expressions."[72]

Merger principles have been applied to computer software, for example, where efficiency concerns narrow the "practical range of choice."[73] If a "particular set of modules is necessary efficiently to implement that part of the program's process being implemented . . . then the expression represented by the programmer's choice of a specific module or group of modules has merged with their underlying idea and is unprotected."[74] It may be that there is only one or a limited number of ways to optimally write code to carry out a particular process—for example, a "bubble sort" algorithm.[75] In those cases, the expression merges with the method, and the expression cannot be copyrighted. If, however, there are multiple ways to carry out that process, the merger doctrine would not apply and the author could claim copyright in the expression used to capture the ideas even though the idea itself remained a public good.[76]

Another limitation on copyright is the common law doctrine of *scènes à faire*, which provides that the expressive elements of a work are not entitled to protection if they are standard, stock, or common to a particular topic, or if they necessarily follow from a common theme or setting. Courts have recognized that extending copyright protection to the necessary incidents of a particular theme or setting would grant a monopoly to the first person who adopted that form of expression.[77] In that sense, *scènes à faire* and

---

[71] *Id.* § 13.03[B][3].

[72] GOLDSTEIN ON COPYRIGHT § 2.3.2.

[73] *Comput. Assocs. Int'l, Inc. v. Altai, Inc.,* 982 F.2d 693, 708 (2d Cir. 1992).

[74] *Id.* (emphasis omitted).

[75] A "bubble sort" algorithm is a simple sorting algorithm that, as applied to a list of numbers, makes repeated passes through a list, swapping adjacent numbers if they are in the wrong order. Waldemar Dos Passos, NUMERICAL METHODS, ALGORITHMS AND TOOLS IN C#, at 175 (2010) (describing ways to code a bubble sort algorithm in the C# programming language, of varying degrees of efficiency).

[76] CONTU Report at 20 ("When other language *is* available programmers are free to read copyrighted programs and use the ideas embodied in them in preparing their own works," "but one is not free to take another's program."). There is a divide in the courts—that the Copyright Office does not here express a view on—regarding whether merger goes to the copyrightability of a work or whether it constitutes a defense to infringement. *See Oracle Am., Inc. v. Google Inc.,* 750 F.3d 1339, 1358 (Fed. Cir. 2015) (describing circuit court disagreement); *see also* 4-13 NIMMER ON COPYRIGHT § 13.03[B][3] (concluding that "the better view is to treat the merger doctrine under the rubric of substantial similarity, evaluating the inseparability of idea and expression in the context of a particular dispute, rather than attempting to disqualify certain expressions from protection *per se*").

[77] *See, e.g., CMM Cable Rep, Inc. v. Ocean Coast Props., Inc.,* 97 F.3d 1504, 1522 n.25 (1st Cir. 1996) (noting that *scènes à faire* is "concerned with preventing a monopoly on commonplace ideas").

merger both serve the same purpose by limiting the scope of an author's copyright where there are limited ways to express a particular idea.

For both merger and *scènes à faire*, courts must focus on the options available to the author at the time a work is initially created, rather than the choices available to users after the fact.[78] Indeed, this view is compelled by section 302(a) of the Copyright Act, which provides that copyright in a work created on or after January 1, 1978 "subsists from its creation and . . . endures" during the term prescribed by the statute.[79]

Although courts first applied *scènes à faire* in cases involving dramatic works, the doctrine has been extended to computer programs. For example, courts have recognized that *scènes à faire* may limit or even eliminate protection for elements of a program that are dictated by external factors, such as: the mechanical specifications of the computer running the program; compatibility requirements of other programs with which the program is intended to operate; hardware design standards that have been adopted by computer manufacturers; widely accepted programming techniques within the computer industry; as well as the demands of the industry that is expected to use the program.[80]

In *Lexmark International, Inc. v. Static Control Components, Inc.*, a case concerning interoperability of software contained in printer toner cartridges, the Sixth Circuit employed elements of both merger and *scènes à faire* analysis in assessing the copyrightability of a "toner loading" program.[81] The court concluded that the program lacked sufficient originality to qualify for protection, given the uncontested evidence that the program "as it [was] written [was] the most straightforward, efficient, natural way to express the program,"[82] "that functionality and efficiency considerations

---

[78] *See Oracle Am., Inc.*, 750 F.3d at 1361 ("It is well-established that copyrightability and the scope of protectable activity are to be evaluated at the time of creation, not at the time of infringement."); *id.* at 1364 (explaining that "the focus of the [*scènes à faire*] doctrine is on the circumstances presented to the creator, not the copier"); *Dun & Bradstreet Software v. Grace Consulting*, 307 F.3d 197, 215 (3d Cir. 2002) ("[I]n determining whether certain aspects of an allegedly infringed software are not protected by copyright law [under *scènes à faire*], the focus is on external factors that influenced the choice of the creator of the infringed product."); *see also Mitel, Inc. v. Iqtel, Inc.*, 124 F.3d 1366, 1375 (10th Cir. 1997) (finding that the district court's application of the *scènes à faire* doctrine "should have remained upon the external factors that dictated [the plaintiff's]" creation of the work, instead of focusing on "external factors such as market forces and efficiency considerations" justifying the defendant's copying).

[79] 17 U.S.C. § 302.

[80] *See, e.g., Comput. Mgmt. Assistance Co. v. Robert F. DeCastro, Inc.*, 220 F.3d 396, 401-02 (5th Cir. 2000) (considering stock industry demands in connection with program for tracking orders, inventory, and promotional pricing); *Mitel, Inc.*, 124 F.3d at 1374-75 (addressing hardware compatibility requirements and industry practices); *Comput. Assocs. Int'l*, 982 F.2d at 709, 715 (outlining doctrine in context of programmed organizational charts).

[81] *Lexmark Int'l, Inc. v. Static Control Components, Inc.*, 387 F.3d 522, 537-43 (6th Cir. 2004).

[82] *Id.* at 540 (citation omitted).

precluded any material changes,"[83] and that the program was "a no-thought translation of the formulas to the language that the internal loading program must be written in."[84] In short, the court concluded that these constraints left the programmer without "much choice" in how to write the program.[85]

As commenters acknowledged, application of these doctrines may be difficult in practice.[86] The toner loading program at issue in *Lexmark* was an exceedingly short program[87] that Lexmark had included with its printer toner cartridges, and the program's brevity and simplicity may have contributed substantially to the court's findings. Nonetheless, these doctrines are likely to have particular force with respect to the kinds of highly functional embedded software described in Part II above.

The applicability of the merger and *scènes à faire* in the context of embedded software is addressed in greater depth in Parts IV.B, C, and D below.

3. Fair Use

Fair use was initially a judicial creation, but in 1978 Congress codified it in section 107 of the Copyright Act, providing general guidance flexible enough to handle a wide variety of factual scenarios. Section 107 allows for the fair use of copyrighted works, and provides a list of paradigmatic fair use purposes, specifically "criticism, comment, news reporting, teaching (including multiple copies for classroom use), scholarship, or research."[88] To aid the determination of whether a use is fair, the Copyright Act provides four non-exhaustive factors: (1) the purpose and character of the use, including whether such use is of a commercial nature or is for nonprofit educational purposes; (2) the nature of the copyrighted work; (3) the amount and substantiality of the portion used in relation to the copyrighted work as a whole; and (4) the effect of the use upon the potential market for or value of the copyrighted work.[89]

Courts have regularly applied the fair use doctrine in the context of software. For example, courts have permitted uses of software ensuring interoperability with new products and devices. In *Sega Enterprises Ltd. v. Accolade, Inc.*, the court held that

---

[83] *Id.* at 539.

[84] *Id.* at 540 (citation omitted).

[85] *Id.*

[86] *See, e.g.*, Tr. at 21:23-22:06 (May 24, 2016) (Ashley Ailsworth, SEMA) (explaining that it is hard to distinguish expressive elements from non-expressive elements).

[87] The court noted that the two versions of the program were 37 and 55 bytes each, which is less than the space needed to store "the phrase 'Lexmark International, Inc. vs. Static Control Components, Inc.'" *Lexmark*, 387 F.3d at 529-30.

[88] 17 U.S.C. § 107.

[89] *Id.* Section 107 of the Copyright Act also provides that "[t]he fact that a work is unpublished shall not itself bar a finding of fair use if such finding is made upon consideration of all the above factors." *Id.*

copying a video game console's computer program to decompile and reverse engineer the object code to make it interoperable with the defendant's video games was a fair use.[90] Similarly, in *Sony Computer Entertainment, Inc. v. Connectix Corp.*, the court held that reverse engineering the operating system of a PlayStation gaming console to develop a computer program allowing users to play PlayStation video games on a desktop computer, as well as making copies in the course of such reverse engineering, was a fair use.[91]

Specific applications of the fair use doctrine are addressed in Parts IV.B, C, and D below.

4. First Sale Doctrine

Codified in section 109 of the Copyright Act, the first sale doctrine states that "the owner of a particular copy or phonorecord lawfully made under this title, or any person authorized by such owner, is entitled, without the authority of the copyright owner, to sell or otherwise dispose of the possession of that copy or phonorecord."[92] This language is subject to additional conditions, including a restriction on renting, leasing, or lending computer programs in certain situations.[93] Importantly, section 109(a) is limited to the "*owner* of a particular copy." Software companies often use licensing models for distribution of their software, which can call into question whether the possessor of a copy of a computer program would be considered the "owner" under the first sale doctrine in practice.[94]

The applicability of the first sale doctrine in the context of embedded software is addressed in greater depth in Part IV.A below.

5. Section 117

In section 117, the Copyright Act provides a number of limitations on exclusive rights for computer programs. Section 117(a) allows copies or adaptations of computer programs to be made either "as an essential step in the utilization of the computer program in conjunction with a machine" or for archival purposes.[95] It also allows for the

---

[90] 977 F.2d 1510, 1527-28 (9th Cir. 1992), *amended by* 1993 U.S. App. LEXIS 78 (9th Cir. Jan. 6, 1993).

[91] 203 F.3d 596, 608 (9th Cir. 2000).

[92] 17 U.S.C. § 109.

[93] For an extensive discussion of the history of section 109, *see* U.S. COPYRIGHT OFFICE, DMCA SECTION 104 REPORT 19-25 (2001), https://www.copyright.gov/reports/studies/dmca/sec-104-report-vol-1.pdf ("DMCA SECTION 104 REPORT"). Additionally, section 109 limits the first sale doctrine regarding restored works under the Uruguay Round Agreements Act. 17 U.S.C. § 109(a); *see also* Uruguay Round Agreements Act, Pub. L. No. 103-465, § 514, 108 Stat. 4809, 4981 (1994).

[94] *See* DEP'T OF COMMERCE INTERNET POLICY TASK FORCE, WHITE PAPER ON REMIXES, FIRST SALE, AND STATUTORY DAMAGES 64-65 (2016), https://www.uspto.gov/sites/default/files/documents/copyrightwhitepaper.pdf ("INTERNET POLICY TASK FORCE WHITE PAPER").

[95] 17 U.S.C. § 117(a)(1)-(2).

transfer of any copies prepared in accordance with the exceptions, though adaptations may only be transferred with the authorization of the copyright owner.[96] Section 117(a), like the provision regarding first sale, may only be invoked by "the owner of a copy of a computer program."[97] This raises complex questions regarding whether a consumer owns a copy of software installed on a device or machine for purposes of section 117(a) when formal title is lacking or a license purports to impose restrictions on the use of the computer program.[98] The general legal principles involving the ownership versus licensing question are addressed in detail in the following section. In addition, section 117(b) places some limitations on the subsequent lease, sale, or transfer of copies made lawfully under section 117.[99]

Congress enacted sections 117(c) and (d) to provide a specific defense to "ensure that independent service organizations do not inadvertently become liable for copyright infringement merely because they have turned on a machine in order to service its hardware components."[100] Congress enacted these provisions after the Ninth Circuit, in *MAI Systems Corp. v. Peak Computer, Inc.*, held that a computer repair technician who loaded software programs into random access memory ("RAM") without authorization committed copyright infringement.[101]

---

[96] Act of Dec. 12, 1980, Pub. L. No. 96-517,§ 10, 94 Stat. 3015, 3029 (1980).

[97] 17 U.S.C. § 117(a). In enacting this provision, Congress largely adopted the language proposed by CONTU, with one exception. The original report would have made the section 117(a) exception available to any "rightful possessor" of a copy. CONTU Report at 12. Congress changed the language from "rightful possessor" to "owner," without explanation. *See* H.R. REP. NO. 96-1307(I), at 23 (1980) *reprinted in* 1980 U.S.C.C.A.N. 6460, 6482. Courts have attached varying degrees of significance to this change. *See generally Krause v. Titleserv, Inc.*, 402 F.3d 119, 122-23 (2d Cir. 2005).

[98] *See Vernor v. Autodesk, Inc.*, 621 F.3d 1102, 1111 (9th Cir. 2010); *Krause*, 402 F.3d at 124.

[99] 17 U.S.C. § 117(b) (providing that "exact copies" made lawfully under section 117 may be "leased, sold, or otherwise transferred . . . only as part of the lease, sale, or other transfer of all rights in the program" and that "[a]daptations" made under the section "may be transferred only with the authorization of the copyright owner"). Sections 117(a) and (b) were added to the Copyright Act as part of 1980 amendments implementing CONTU's recommendations. Act of Dec. 12, 1980, Pub. L. No. 96-517, § 10, 94 Stat. 3015, 3028-29.

[100] *See* H.R. REP. NO. 105-551 at 27.

[101] 991 F.2d 511, 519 (9th Cir. 1993). The "RAM copy doctrine" was subject to significant critique in this study. *See, e.g.*, Aaron Perzanowski et al. Initial Comments at 3 (urging that the RAM copy doctrine "has cast the shadow of infringement liability over nearly every use—personal and commercial, private and public—of a digital work"). This issue was addressed in detail by the Copyright Office in a 2001 report, which recommended "against the adoption of a general exception from the reproduction right to render noninfringing all temporary copies that are incidental to lawful uses." DMCA SECTION 104 REPORT 141. It appears that the RAM copy doctrine is today firmly established as a matter of case law. *See, e.g., MDY Indus., LLC v. Blizzard Entm't, Inc.*, 629 F.3d 928, 938-39 (9th Cir. 2011); *Stenograph L.L.C. v. Bossard Assocs., Inc.*, 144 F.3d 96, 101-02 (D.C. Cir. 1998). Reconsideration of the doctrine—which applies to all software, not just software embedded in consumer products—is beyond the scope of this study.

Thus, section 117(c) states that "the owner or lessee of a machine . . . that lawfully contains an authorized copy of a computer program" may make (or authorize a third party to make) a copy of a computer program "if such copy is made solely by virtue of the activation of a machine that lawfully contains an authorized copy of the computer program," provided that the copy is made for purposes "of maintenance or repair of that machine."[102] Notably, section 117(c) applies regardless of whether the owner of the device "owns" the copy of the programs that are embedded within that device.

Section 117(d), in turn, specifies that "maintenance" of a machine is the "servicing of the machine in order to make it work in accordance with its original specifications and any changes to those specifications authorized for that machine," while "repair" of a machine "is the restoring of the machine to the state of working in accordance with its original specifications and any changes to those specifications authorized for that machine."[103]

The applicability of these provisions in the context of embedded software is addressed in greater depth in Parts IV.B and C below.

6.   *De Minimis* Uses

A number of courts have recognized that *de minimis* uses of copyrighted computer programs are not infringing. Though difficult to define in the abstract, a *de minimis* use is one that is trivial.[104] As the Second Circuit observed, "[b]ecause of the *de minimis* doctrine, in trivial instances of copying, we are in fact not breaking the law . . . because trivial copying is not an infringement."[105] It is important to note, however, that the "de minimis defense does not apply where the qualitative value of the copying is material."[106]

Similarly, although modifying code may implicate the derivative work right in section 106(2), it may be that the changes are so minimal that the new works do not implicate that right at all.[107]

---

[102] 17 U.S.C. § 117(c).

[103] *Id.* § 117(d)

[104] *Davis v. Gap, Inc.*, 246 F.3d 152, 173 (2d Cir. 2001).

[105] *Id.*

[106] *Dun & Bradstreet Software Servs., Inc.*, 307 F.3d at 208.

[107] *See generally* COMPENDIUM (THIRD) § 311.2. *See also Lewis Galoob Toys, Inc. v. Nintendo of Am., Inc.*, 964 F.2d 965, 969 (9th Cir. 1992) (holding the GameGenie system, which simply modified the output of a computer program, did not result in a derivative work). *Compare Midway Mfg. Co. v. Arctic Int'l, Inc.*, 704 F.2d 1009, 1014 (7th Cir. 1983) (holding that a modified version of a video game constituted a derivative work).

C.   Ownership versus Licensing

A significant issue arising in the context of software in general, and software-enabled consumer products in particular, is the question of when copies of software are "owned" or, instead, "licensed" for purposes of the Copyright Act. As explained above, section 117(a) and the first sale doctrine in section 109 both turn on whether one is the "owner of a particular copy," meaning that licensees cannot take advantage of the exceptions provided by section 117(a) and the first sale doctrine.[108]

Copies of software are commonly distributed subject to the purchaser's consent to the terms of a written agreement, particularly when sold as standalone products.[109] Those terms can vary greatly based on the kind of software at issue. Some software is accompanied by what is called an "end-user license agreement," or "EULA," which imposes restrictive terms on the use of the software. Although the practice of requiring consent to a license agreement is virtually uniform with respect to software that is sold as a standalone product, it appears to be less common with respect to many kinds of software-enabled consumer products.[110] In those cases, the consumer can often be said to "own" the copy of the software.[111] As discussed in Part IV.E below, however, there are at least some software-enabled consumer products that are sold with a license.

As an initial matter, some commenters argued that copies of software can *never* be licensed. They reached that conclusion on two somewhat different statutory grounds. First, a group of law professors argued that section 106(3) exclusively defines "the types of transactions available to copyright holders under the exclusive right to distribution,"

---

[108] *See* 17 U.S.C. §§ 109(a), 117(a).

[109] *See, e.g.*, Copyright Alliance Initial Comments at 9 ("The software industry has relied for decades on a licensing model for the distribution, maintenance, and updating of its software products and services to and for its customers . . . . [S]oftware is virtually always licensed and not sold . . . ."); ACT Initial Comments at 9 ("Many copyrighted products, including apps, are distributed subject to license agreements that use 'click-through' agreements facilitated by the app store platform (*e.g.*, iOS)."); ESA Initial Comments at 12 ("Software is commonly licensed, including sometimes, embedded software."); SIIA Initial Comments at 4 & n.3 ("Most SIIA members license their products . . . . Licensing is the dominant method of software distribution."). *See also Apple, Inc. v. Psystar Corp.*, 658 F.3d 1150, 1155 (9th Cir. 2011) (noting that "[s]oftware license agreements . . . have become ubiquitous in the software industry").

[110] *See* U.S. COPYRIGHT OFFICE, SECTION 1201 RULEMAKING: SIXTH TRIENNIAL PROCEEDING TO DETERMINE EXEMPTIONS TO THE PROHIBITION ON CIRCUMVENTION 287 (Oct. 2015), https://www.copyright.gov/1201/2015/registers-recommendation.pdf ("2015 SECTION 1201 RECOMMENDATION") (discussing lack of written license agreements involving vehicle ECU software).

[111] When formal title is lacking and a copyright owner transfers a product containing a copyrighted work, the circumstances of that transaction will dictate whether the transferee is an "owner" of the copy of the work. The two leading precedents both reflect in their separate tests that the possessor of that product would likely be considered an "owner" of the software copy if the copyright owner places no restrictions on the consumers' use or resale of that work. *See Vernor*, 621 F.3d at 1111; *Krause*, 402 F.3d. at 124. For a further discussion of this issue regarding ownership, *see* Part IV.A.

because the provision only describes distributions "by sale or other transfer of ownership, or by rental, lease, or lending."[112] Thus, in this view, because "every distribution of a copy is either a transfer of ownership or it's a rental, a lease or a lending," "[t]he idea of a licensed copy is really a myth."[113] Second, in a joint comment, two public advocacy organizations asserted that the concept of "licensing" software is undermined by the fact that the Copyright Act defines copies to be "'material objects . . . in which a work is fixed . . . .'"[114] Thus, they reason, "[a] person who owns the material object in which a copy is embedded necessarily owns a copy of the copyrighted work."[115]

These arguments, at present, run counter to a uniform line of case law recognizing that copies of software can be "licensed" within the meaning of the Copyright Act.[116] Thus, in the Copyright Office's view, the more critical issue is how courts should assess the question of ownership versus licensing under the existing case law.

The two leading cases, *Krause v. Titleserv, Inc.*[117] and *Vernor v. Autodesk, Inc.*,[118] describe tests that provide some guidance in determining whether a transaction can be characterized as a sale or a license.

In *Krause*, the plaintiff Krause wrote computer programs for the defendant Titleserv that were installed on Titleserv's computer network to be accessible to employees.[119] Krause terminated his relationship with Titleserv, leaving copies of the source code for some of the programs and executable versions of all of the programs on Titleserv's file servers.[120] Titleserv's employees modified the source code to fix bugs, add new customers, and

---

[112] Aaron Perzanowski et al. Initial Comments at 4 (quoting 17 U.S.C. § 106(3)).

[113] Tr. at 98:05-14 (May 18, 2016) (Aaron Perzanowski, Case Western Reserve University School of Law). *See also* Aaron Perzanowski et al. Initial Comments at 4 ("[T]here is no free-standing transactional form called a 'license' when it comes to the transfer of particular copies, such as those embedded in a phone, watch, or tractor.").

[114] Public Knowledge/OTI Initial Comments at 3 (quoting 17 U.S.C. § 101 (definition of "copies")).

[115] *Id.*

[116] *See, e.g., Adobe Sys. Inc. v. Christenson*, 809 F.3d 1071, 1077-79 (9th Cir. 2015) (discussing the issue at length); *Vernor*, 621 F.3d at 1110-11; *DSC Commc'ns Corp. v. Pulse Commc'ns, Inc.*, 170 F.3d 1354, 1361-62 (Fed. Cir. 1999). Indeed, the Supreme Court appears to have validated this understanding of the Act. *See Quality King Distribs., Inc. v. L'Anza Research Int'l, Inc.*, 523 U.S. 135, 147 (1998) (noting that "because the protection afforded by § 109(a) is available only to the 'owner' of a lawfully made copy (or someone authorized by the owner), the first sale doctrine would not provide a defense . . . against any nonowner such as a bailee, *a licensee*, a consignee, or one whose possession of the copy was unlawful") (emphasis added).

[117] 402 F.3d 119 (2d Cir. 2005).

[118] 621 F.3d 1102 (9th Cir. 2010).

[119] *Krause*, 402 F.3d at 120.

[120] *Id.* at 120-21.

change customer addresses "to keep the old programs functional."[121] Krause subsequently brought suit against Titleserv alleging copyright infringement, and Titleserv defended by arguing that its modifications of Krause's programs were noninfringing under section 117(a).[122]

On appeal, the Second Circuit held that "formal title in a program copy is not an absolute prerequisite to qualifying for § 117(a)'s affirmative defense," but rather that "courts should inquire into whether the party exercises sufficient incidents of ownership over a copy of the program to be sensibly considered the owner of the copy."[123] The court concluded that Titleserv owned the copies of the program, reaching its conclusion after considering the following factors in the aggregate:

> Titleserv paid Krause substantial consideration to develop the programs for its sole benefit. Krause customized the software to serve Titleserv's operations. The copies were stored on a server owned by Titleserv. Krause never reserved the right to repossess the copies used by Titleserv and agreed that Titleserv had the right to continue to possess and use the programs forever, regardless whether its relationship with Krause terminated. Titleserv was similarly free to discard or destroy the copies any time it wished.[124]

Notably, there was no evidence of a *written* license agreement; rather, Krause's claim was that Titleserv "possessed the copies as a licensee pursuant to an oral agreement."[125] The court, however, found that none of the oral statements Krause pointed to showed the existence of a license arrangement; rather, the statements "relate[d] to the ownership and/or right to use of the copyright, and not to ownership of the copies."[126]

In *Vernor*, Autodesk produced a piece of software called AutoCAD Release 14 software ("Release 14"), a "computer-aided design software used by architects, engineers, and manufacturers."[127] Autodesk offered Release 14 to its customers pursuant to a written license agreement requiring acceptance before installation.[128] The license agreement had various detailed restrictions: providing that Autodesk retained title to all copies; stating that the customer had a nonexclusive and nontransferable license to use the software; restricting transfer of the software without Autodesk's prior consent; imposing use

---

[121] *Id.* at 121.

[122] *Id.*

[123] *Id.* at 124.

[124] *Id.*

[125] *Id.* at 122.

[126] *Id.* at 124.

[127] *Vernor*, 621 F.3d at 1104.

[128] *Id.*

restrictions, such as prohibiting modification, translation or reverse-engineering; and providing for license termination where the user copied the software without authorization or otherwise did not comply with the license.[129]

Vernor purchased used copies of Release 14 from a variety of unauthorized sellers, including one of Autodesk's direct customers, Cardwell/Thomas & Associates ("CTA"). Vernor subsequently resold the copies on eBay.[130] After Autodesk was made aware of the fact that copies of Release 14 were being sold on eBay, it filed DMCA take-down notices with eBay and directed Vernor to stop selling the software.[131] In response, Vernor brought a declaratory judgment action against Autodesk, arguing that his resale of copies of Release 14 was protected by the first sale doctrine in section 109 and the essential step defense in section 117(a).[132]

On appeal, the Ninth Circuit determined that the affirmative defenses provided by the first sale doctrine and the essential step defense are "unavailable to those who are only licensed to use their copies of copyrighted works," and that the salient inquiry in this case was "whether Autodesk sold Release 14 copies to its customers or licensed the copies to its customers."[133] After considering Ninth Circuit precedent, the court determined that "a software user is a licensee rather than an owner of a copy where the copyright owner: (1) specifies that the user is granted a license; (2) significantly restricts the user's ability to transfer the software; and (3) imposes notable use restrictions."[134] Using these factors, the court held that "CTA was a licensee rather than an owner of copies of Release 14 and thus was not entitled to invoke the first sale doctrine or the essential step defense,"[135] because "Autodesk reserved title to Release 14 copies and imposed significant transfer and use restrictions."[136] Consequently, "Vernor [also] did not receive title to the copies from CTA and accordingly could not pass ownership on to others."[137]

Some commenters have asserted that *Krause* and *Vernor* present two very different and, more importantly, conflicting tests,[138] and in some cases have indicated that one is more

---

[129] *Id.*

[130] *Id.* at 1103.

[131] *Id.* at 1105-06.

[132] *Id.* at 1106.

[133] *Id.* at 1107.

[134] *Id.* at 1111.

[135] *Id.*

[136] *Id.* at 1112.

[137] *Id.*

[138] *See, e.g.*, EFF Initial Comments at 7 (asserting that "[t]he split between *Krause* and *Vernor* could lead to very different results in the context of software-enabled devices"); Owners' Rights Initiative Initial

correct than the other.[139] *Krause* and *Vernor*, however, ultimately both turn on the courts' differing assessments of the nature of the transaction between the parties, including the level of control the copyright owner asserted over the copy of software. Ultimately, the Copyright Office believes that the opposing outcomes in *Krause* and *Vernor* are the result of the significantly different facts and circumstances presented in those cases, rather than the somewhat different contours of the courts' analyses.

D.   Other Areas of Law

The Committee also asked the Copyright Office to "identify key issues in how the copyright law intersects with other areas of law in establishing how products that rely on software to function can be lawfully used."[140] State contract law is of particular salience here, as software-enabled everyday products are sometimes distributed with licenses restricting the use of the included software. This issue is addressed in detail in Part IV.E below.

Commenters and the Copyright Office identified a number of other non-copyright laws that may affect the use of software-enabled everyday products, although further analysis of the scope and propriety of their reach is generally beyond the scope of this study. For instance, patent, trademark, and unfair competition law may be relevant to assessing the scope of legal protection of embedded software.[141] Laws prohibiting false advertising may also be relevant. Commenters expressed the concern that manufacturers of software-enabled consumer products may be engaging in false advertising and "misleading consumers about the fundamental nature of the transaction," by "characterizing transactions as sales or purchases [in advertising or labeling] when, in fact, the fine print imposes significant and unexpected limitations."[142]

Additionally, commenters raised concerns about the effectiveness of consumer protection laws and, in particular, the ability for vendors in the software industry to "disclaim liability for defects in their products through boilerplate language in sales contracts and licensing agreements . . . . [allowing them] to exempt themselves from

---

Comments at 6 (citing *Krause* and *Vernor*, and pointing out that "U.S. circuit courts are split on . . . . whether a person who acquires a copy of a computer program is an owner or a licensee of the copy").

[139] *See, e.g.,* EFF Initial Comments at 7 (stating that the "*Vernor* approach should be repudiated at the national level"); Aaron Perzanowski et al. Initial Comments at 11 (arguing that the court in *Krause* "look[ed] to the economic reality of a transaction rather than the self-serving language of license terms drafted by copyright holders").

[140] Grassley/Leahy Letter at 2.

[141] *See, e.g., Alice Corp. Pty. Ltd. v. CLS Bank Int'l,* 134 S. Ct. 2347 (2014) (patent); *Checkpoint Sys. v. Check Point Software Techs. Inc.,* 269 F.3d 270 (3d Cir. 2001) (trademark).

[142] Aaron Perzanowski et al. Initial Comments at 11. *See also* Tr. at 131:04-07 (May 18, 2016) (Aaron Perzanowski, Case Western Reserve University School of Law) (asserting that "these kind of false advertising concerns that I've raised are legally distinct from the kinds of question that we're trying to answer here").

consumer protection laws that are otherwise universally applicable."[143] There also were concerns over such language being used by manufacturers to evade tort liability.[144]

Finally, some commenters identified privacy concerns, either as a reason for allowing manufacturers to impose licenses on consumers to ensure data protection,[145] or as a reason for nullifying such licenses to provide consumers more control over whether and how manufacturers collect their personal information.[146]

The Copyright Office notes that many of these issues also arise with respect to the Internet of Things, a subset of software-enabled products that "connect, communicate or transmit information with or between each other through the Internet."[147] Like the software at issue in this study, the Internet of Things raises a variety of privacy and security issues, which have been studied by other components of the U.S. government, including the Federal Trade Commission, the Department of Homeland Security, and Department of Commerce's Internet Policy Task Force.[148]

---

[143] Public Knowledge/OTI Initial Comments at 10. *See also* Tr. at 26:02-04 (May 18, 2016) (John Bergmayer, Public Knowledge) ("I don't think that it is copyright law that should really be part of the discussion in terms of those sorts of consumer protection.").

[144] *See, e.g.*, Public Knowledge/OTI Initial Comments at 10 (asserting that, with respect to tort liability, "[a] manufacturer or seller should not be able to evade what would otherwise be their responsibilities under the law merely because their products now contain software," as doing so would "nullify decades of statutory and common law protections that were designed to protect consumers from poorly-designed or defective products and negligent commercial practices"). *But see* Tr. at 40:06-14 (May 18, 2016) (Chris Mohr, SIIA) ("Product liability is a tort and it's a tort under state law. . . . [A tort] is not going to be governed by the terms of a license agreement because . . . that's a very different type of analysis.").

[145] *See* ACT Initial Comments at 9 (asserting that "[a]dherence to licensing terms, for example, is crucial to ensuring data integrity and resiliency, as well as end user privacy"); Tr. at 17:06-12 (May 24, 2016) (Evan Cox, BSA) (stating that with these devices, "you're dealing more with a service relationship, which there's ongoing updating and interacting with software, a lot of liability and burdens on the provider of that software as a service, including liability concerns, security concerns, privacy breach concerns").

[146] *See* KEI Initial Comments at 4 (asserting that licenses attached to software-enabled consumer products "allow businesses to set the terms of what information is collected about users, and how that information is distributed and used," and that "[t]here are legitimate concerns that consumer privacy may be abused by third parties that have access to data collected in the course of use of a software-enabled consumer product, or that such data may be compromised by other malicious parties").

[147] FEDERAL TRADE COMMISSION, INTERNET OF THINGS, PRIVACY AND SECURITY IN A CONNECTED WORLD 6 (2015), *available at* https://www.ftc.gov/system/files/documents/reports/federal-trade-commission-staff-report-november-2013-workshop-entitled-internet-things-privacy/150127iotrpt.pdf.

[148]*Internet of Things*, NAT'L TELECOMM. & INFO. ADMIN., https://www.ntia.doc.gov/category/internet-things; *Securing the Internet of Things*, DEP'T OF HOMELAND SECURITY, https://www.dhs.gov/securingtheIoT; INTERNET OF THINGS: PRIVACY AND SECURITY IN A CONNECTED WORLD, *supra* note 147. .

IV.   Analysis of Specific Concerns Raised by Software-Enabled Consumer Products

The Committee asked the Copyright Office to study the extent to which "the design, distribution, and legitimate uses of products" and "innovative services" are being "enabled and/or frustrated by the application of existing copyright law to software in everyday products."[149] In addition, the Committee asked the Office to analyze how such products "can be lawfully used" in light of the ways "copyright law intersects with other areas of law."[150]

Software-enabled consumer products, while subject to general copyright law, can pose a range of special challenges in these areas. These include issues related to resale and repair, security research, interoperability, and the licensing of embedded software. As discussed below, because existing legal doctrines—including the idea/expression dichotomy, merger, *scènes à faire*, section 117, and fair use—are well-suited to address some of these concerns, the Copyright Office does not believe any legislative changes are necessary at this time.

To be sure, to those seeking to engage in these legitimate activities, relying on these somewhat indeterminate doctrines brings less certainty than would bright-line legislative fixes. Indeed, some of these issues may have to be resolved through litigation, which carries obvious risks. But legislation carries its own risks in the specific context of the products at issue in this Report because, among other things, the technology in these products is evolving so rapidly. Legislation thus can be underinclusive—addressing the technologies of today but failing to anticipate the different technologies of tomorrow. In that respect, what the established legal doctrines lack in determinacy, they make up for in flexibility; they can be—and have been— extended and applied to new technologies as they have developed. Furthermore, this Report itself can serve as a roadmap of sorts for those seeking to make legitimate use of embedded software. For these reasons, the Copyright Office is confident that U.S. copyright law can maintain an appropriate balance and guide the lawful use of embedded software.

A.   Resale

The increased inclusion of embedded software in consumer products raises the issue of whether and how consumers can resell or otherwise transfer such products.[151] Some

---

[149] Grassley/Leahy Letter at 2.

[150] *Id.*

[151] To be clear, this analysis is limited to embedded software like that described in Part II; the Office is not here assessing questions of when a device containing other copyrighted works—like music, movies, or apps—can be resold under section 109. The Department of Commerce's Internet Policy Task Force observed

products traditionally resold without restriction, such as cars, now include embedded software, and consumer groups have voiced concerns over whether section 109's first sale doctrine permits the resale of that software when the product itself is resold.[152]

As noted above, the first sale right only applies to the "owner of a particular copy."[153] Does the owner of a car also "own" the particular copies of software that are embedded in that car for purposes of exercising the first sale right? A number of commenters expressed concern that, under current law, the answer to that question might be "no," especially in light of licensing practices for standalone software.[154] Another concern was that license agreements may only provide software updates such as security patches to the original licensee, and will withhold them from downstream purchasers.[155] As a result, these commenters worried about the use of copyright law to encroach on established consumer rights and expectations.[156]

As an initial matter, as noted in Part III.C above, many software-enabled consumer products are not sold with written license agreements at all. For instance, during the most recent section 1201 triennial rulemaking proceeding, representatives of auto manufacturers "conceded . . . that with the exception of the software controlling the entertainment and telematics systems, ECU [electronic control unit] software is not subject to written licensing agreements."[157] In such cases, there should be no question

---

earlier this year: "In the case of devices containing downloads of copies of works, when the downloading is performed under a license, there may be policy reasons not to allow resale. . . . [I]t is common for licenses for music, books, and movies to permit the licensee to make multiple copies on multiple devices for her own personal use, or to share copies with others. Such licenses may also forbid the licensee to transfer the downloaded copy, even as part of a transfer of the consumer product onto which the copy was downloaded." INTERNET POLICY TASK FORCE WHITE PAPER at 64.

[152] *See, e.g.*, CCIA Initial Comments at 2 ("Product licensing agreements for goods with embedded software may attempt to restrict lawful transfers or resale of lawfully acquired products, impairing economically desirable transactions between consumers and secondary buyers.").

[153] 17 U.S.C. § 109.

[154] *See* Auto Care Ass'n Initial Comments at 6 (noting that original equipment managers make "extravagant claims [in the press] that the first sale doctrine cannot apply because consumers merely 'license' and do not own the copy of the software embedded in vehicle parts").

[155] Owners' Rights Initiative Initial Comments at 4 (asserting that "Oracle refuses to supply routine updates to the purchasers of used hardware products containing essential Oracle software, unless they make an additional payment").

[156] Engine Advocacy Initial Comments at 10 ("Owners have almost always enjoyed the right and ability to . . . sell devices and other property they have purchased."); Aaron Perzanowski et al. Initial Comments at 9 (noting that "when a consumer buys a car, a phone, or a pacemaker, they expect to own it . . . includ[ing] the software that is equally, if not more, responsible for the device's characteristics, features, and performance"); EFF Initial Comments at 2 ("Traditionally, once a person has purchased a product, she has been free to use it however she sees fit."); Consumers Union Reply Comments at 2 ("A consumer who purchases a product or otherwise lawfully acquires it should own it, and be able to use it—as he or she sees fit.").

[157] 2015 SECTION 1201 RECOMMENDATION at 287.

that the purchaser of that product also "owns" the copy of the software embedded in the product, and would be entitled to dispose of the product consistent with the requirements of the first sale doctrine.[158]

Furthermore, even where there is a written license agreement accompanying the sale of a software-enabled consumer product, the owner of the product may also be deemed to "own" the copy of the software embedded in that product for purposes of section 109. As discussed above, the determination of whether the software copy is owned or licensed turns on the nature of the transaction between the parties. Under both the *Vernor* and *Krause* decisions, a key part of the inquiry is whether the purchaser has the right to possess and use the product and its embedded software indefinitely and without restriction.[159] In cases where license agreements do not impose *any* restrictions on resale or transfer of the software-enabled product, it seems likely that a court would conclude that the software was owned rather than licensed.[160]

Although commenters made various claims regarding the prevalence of licensing terms restricting the ability for consumers to resell or transfer their copies of software or the products in which such software are embedded, the Copyright Office saw little evidence to substantiate those claims. The Department of Commerce's Internet Policy Task Force reached the same conclusion earlier this year.[161] And while the Office agrees that the ability of downstream purchasers of software-enabled consumer products to obtain security updates after transfer is important, the Copyright Office again did not find evidence that the kinds of products that are the focus of this Report are subject to such limitations. The evidence provided to support the assertion that manufacturers are restricting the resale of software-enabled products involved licenses for enterprise-level products (such as the products of NetApp, Oracle, Palo Alto Networks, and EMC),

---

[158] *See id.* at 304 (discussing effect of lack of written license agreements involving vehicle ECU software).

[159] *See Vernor*, 621 F.3d at 1111 (asking whether the copyright owner "significantly restricts the user's ability to transfer the software" and "imposes notable use restrictions"); *Krause*, 402 F.3d. at 124 (noting that "Krause never reserved the right to repossess the copies used by Titleserv and agreed that Titleserv had the right to continue to possess and use the programs forever, regardless whether its relationship with Krause terminated" and that "Titleserv was similarly free to discard or destroy the copies any time it wished").

[160] *See, e.g., Princeton Payment Sols., LLC v. ACI Worldwide, Inc.*, No. 1:13-CV-852, 2014 WL 4104170, at *7 (E.D. Va. Aug. 15, 2014) (holding that defendant was the owner of copy of software installed on defendant's servers where contracts "do not restrict [defendant's] use of the copies" and defendant "was free to discard or destroy the copies any time it wished to do so"); *ZilYen, Inc. v. Rubber Mfrs. Ass'n*, 935 F. Supp. 2d 211, 220 (D.D.C. 2013) (holding that defendant was owner of copies of software where there was "no language in the agreement restricting the defendant's use of the [copies]").

[161] INTERNET POLICY TASK FORCE WHITE at 64 ("The Task Force did not hear evidence that licenses purporting to restrict a consumer's ability to resell have been used with respect to embedded software that operates a functional product, other than a computer or related equipment. Thus, the record before us does not establish that the kinds of consumer products identified above are currently sold subject to such licenses.").

rather than consumer products.[162] These types of products are not purchased by the average consumer, and do not raise the same concerns about the inequality of bargaining power or the enforcement of contracts of adhesion.[163]

Some commenters made the claim that—even if manufacturers of software-enabled products do not currently impose restrictions on resale as part of software licensing agreements—they may do so in the future in an attempt to eliminate secondary markets for software-enabled products.[164] The Copyright Office agrees that if license agreements in the future interfere with consumers' ability to resell or otherwise dispose of their software-enabled products, such a practice would be a concern worthy of legislative attention.[165] One possible solution is YODA,[166] mentioned above, a bill that several commenters supported as a good starting point to resolve concerns regarding the resale or transfer of software-enabled consumer products.[167] At the same time, there may be reasons to think that this issue is unlikely to arise, including that market forces—such as the efforts of consumer advocacy groups to shed light on abusive practices—are a barrier to engaging in behavior of this sort.[168]

Consequently, in light of the present lack of evidence that consumers are unable to resell or otherwise dispose of their software-enabled consumer products, the Copyright Office does not see any need for legislative action on the issue of resale at this time. This is

---

[162] *See* Owners' Rights Initiative Initial Comments at 4-6; Tr. at 47:02-48:08 (May 18, 2016) (Sarang Damle, U.S. Copyright Office and Jonathan Band, Owners' Rights Initiative) (confirming that the relevant products are identified as enterprise-level products).

[163] *Cf.* GIPC Initial Comments at 6 (asserting that "in the business-to-business context, software licenses are commonly the subject of detailed and extensive negotiation between sophisticated parties, including circumstances in which the final product is destined for sale to the public"); *see also* Tr. at 74:15-20 (May 24, 2016) (Kit Walsh, EFF) ("But to honor freedom of contract, if you have parties who are engaging in an actual negotiation, then that's the kind of scenario where you could engage in trading, freedom to operate, as long as it's conspicuous and transparent.").

[164] *See, e.g.,* Aaron Perzanowski et al. Initial Comments at 3 ("[I]f Mattel decides to clamp down on the secondary market for used toys, it could quite simply refuse to grant permission to aftermarket purchasers to load the software that runs the device. For that matter, so could Ford and Volkswagen.").

[165] INTERNET POLICY TASK FORCE WHITE PAPER at 64 ("We do believe . . . that the alienability of everyday functional products is an important issue for consumers. If the market develops so that such devices are commonly sold with restrictions on subsequent purchasers' use of necessary software, further attention would be warranted.").

[166] H.R. 862, 114th Cong. (2015).

[167] *See, e.g.,* CDT Initial Comments at 5; Engine Advocacy Initial Comments at 13; Owners' Rights Initiative Initial Comments at 8; Aaron Perzanowski et al. Initial Comments at 12; Public Knowledge/OTI Initial Comments at 12.

[168] *Cf.* Brian Barrett, *Keurig's My K-Cup Retreat Shows We Can Beat DRM*, WIRED (May 8, 2015), https://www.wired.com/2015/05/keurig-k-cup-drm/ (noting that consumer complaints and consumer advocacy efforts led Keurig to back away from efforts to enforce digital rights management in its coffee machines).

consistent with the recent conclusion of the Internet Policy Task Force with respect to the extension of the first sale doctrine to digitally transmitted goods.[169]

B.   *Repair and Tinkering*

Another concern raised during the study was the potentially negative impact of copyright law on a consumer's ability to repair or tinker with his or her own products. This concern covered a wide swath of potential uses, from individuals who fix or modify their own devices for their personal use, to individuals who want to share their insights on a non-commercial basis, to those who are in the business of repairing embedded software and/or software-enabled products.[170]

Repair and tinkering activities potentially implicate four of the exclusive rights set forth under section 106 of the Copyright Act:

- Section 106(1)'s reproduction right is implicated when a copy of a program is made and transferred into a test environment where it can be further evaluated, as is customary in repair and tinkering.

- Section 106(2)'s right to prepare derivative works potentially is implicated if a user decides to modify the existing code in some respect, add new lines of code, or develop entirely new programs that interoperate with the existing program.

- Section 106(3)'s distribution right is implicated by a user's decision to sell a newly-modified device or replacement part to a third party.

- Section 106(5)'s display right potentially is implicated if a user decides to post code for an embedded program on a website or other public forum (either with or without any modifications that have been made), even if the user posted the information as a way to share insights with consumers who would like to make similar repairs or modifications to their own devices.[171]

---

[169] *See* INTERNET POLICY TASK FORCE WHITE PAPER at 4 (stating that "[a]mending the law to extend the first sale doctrine to digital transmissions of copyrighted works is not advisable at this time" because there was "insufficient evidence to show that there has been a change in circumstances in markets or technology, and the risks to copyright owners' primary markets do not appear to have diminished").

[170] Issues involving the development and distribution of interoperable products and services that interact with existing software-enabled devices are discussed in more detail in Part IV.D.

[171] *See, e.g.*, SEMA Initial Comments at 2-3 ("In the case of reverse engineering vehicle software, analyzing the entire software program may be critical to understand the functionality of the vehicle and, in addition, to determine how much storage is available to support additional functionality. Importantly, access to the entire work is necessary to ensure that modifications in one part of the code will not negatively impact other functionality."); Tr. at 145:14-19, 146:01-03 (May 24, 2016) (Kyle Wiens, iFixit and Repair.org) ("[I]f you have an issue [with a car], the first thing that you might do is re-flash the firmware, . . . take a copy of firmware from another vehicle and put it on that vehicle to see if you can isolate the problem. . . . [But with some

A number of commenters asserted that restrictive licenses prevent consumers from repairing or tinkering with software-enabled products or using independent third parties (as opposed to the manufacturer or authorized repair technician) to do so.[172] During the study, the Copyright Office heard of copyright infringement lawsuits, or threatened lawsuits, against those engaging in repairs.[173] To reduce the risk of suit for copyright infringement, one commenter noted that more expensive repair options may be pursued instead of less expensive—but "riskier"—options.[174]

But the expression of these concerns was not unanimous. Some commenters claimed that the issues raised during the roundtables were hypotheticals and without sufficient evidentiary support to warrant a change to title 17.[175] Others urged against using copyright law to interfere with established "loss leader" business models, where companies sell a product at a loss to stimulate other sales of more profitable goods or services.[176] In addition to disagreement over the factual and policy basis for concern, some commenters urged against legislative action regarding repair and tinkering because Congress already considered many of the existing complexities in 1998 when it amended section 117,[177] and because existing provisions in the Copyright Act, judicial

---

vehicles,] you actually have to extract the firmware from the vehicle, modify the byte code and then re-flash the car with it.").

[172] *See, e.g.*, Static Control Components Initial Comments at 3 ("By the clever use of labels, or packaging instructions, copyright holders can attempt to use their copyrights (or patent holders their patent rights) to prevent the . . . repair of products."); Engine Advocacy Initial Comments at 10-11 ("Where licenses prohibit users from accessing or tinkering with the embedded software in their devices . . . individuals may be frustrated in their ability to explore and make these sorts of valuable improvements to their devices and to achieve new interoperability with other devices.").

[173] *See, e.g.*, Auto Care Ass'n Initial Comments at 5 (stating that "vehicle parts manufacturers and servicers have been sued and threatened with suit for copyright infringement merely for engaging in repairs of software-controlled parts"); Tr. at 49:04-10 (May 18, 2016) (Shaun Bockert, Dorman Products, Inc.) (referencing lawsuit involving Dorman, *see* Am. Compl. and Jury Demand, *General Motors LLC v. Dorman Prods., Inc.*, No. 2:15-cv-12917 (E.D. Mich. Aug. 18, 2015)).

[174] Tr. at 156:04-18 (May 24, 2016) (Kyle Wiens, iFixit and Repair.org) ("[B]ecause we're afraid of the risk . . . we're selling a $300 repair option instead of $100 repair option that we could provide to consumers because of the murkiness of being able to modify hardware that we own.").

[175] *See, e.g.*, Tr. at 34:13-16 (May 18, 2016) (Steve Tepp, GIPC) ("[T]he concerns that are being raised are often hypothetical. . . . Very little of it is traceable actually to copyright law as the problem."); Copyright Alliance Reply Comments at 2 (same).

[176] Tr. at 59:22-60:03 (May 24, 2016) (Evan Cox, BSA) ("[Y]ou got that [product] for a couple hundred dollars because it's a business model that sells that thing as a loss leader. Most of the console game[] makers have sold their consoles at a loss on the presumption that they can use their constellation of legal rights around that device to make money on the back end.").

[177] Copyright Alliance Reply Comments at 6-7 ("These issues are not new ones. Congress considered the issues back in 1998 when it added section 117 and section 1201. The concerns raised by commenters about repair and modifying software seem to be directed to section 1201, and not section 117.").

interpretations, and rulemaking currently strike the correct balance in copyright law regarding repair of software-enabled consumer products.[178]

As discussed more fully below, the Copyright Office finds that current copyright law, properly interpreted, may provide relief for many repair and tinkering activities. Traditional copyright doctrines such as the idea/expression dichotomy, merger, *scènes à faire*, and fair use provide a combined and reasonable defense for many tinkering and repair activities. At this time, the Office is not recommending any modifications to the Copyright Act to address concerns regarding repair and tinkering. Although some commenters pointed to particular license agreements that purport to restrict the purchaser's ability to freely repair or refurbish their product, as more fully discussed in Part IV.E below, such terms may only be enforceable as a matter of contract. If repair activities are authorized as a matter of fair use, or under section 117, it seems likely that users can engage in them without fear of copyright infringement. In addition, market forces may discourage copyright owners from attempting to prevent independent repair activities.[179] Moreover, creating a statutory exception for tinkering or repair would require Congress to create a precise definition of what these types of activities involve and identify the precise situations where "tinkering" and "repair" should be permitted. Given the pace of technological change, there is a risk that any such exception may soon be obsolete.

---

[178] Microsoft Initial Comments at 9 ("This is not to say that tensions in the system never arise. But when they do, existing provisions in the Copyright Act, combined with agency rulemaking, judicial interpretations, and voluntary private-sector efforts, have proven up to the task of maintaining the right balance."); SIIA Initial Comments at 6 ("Issues relating to so-called 'rights to tinker,' the 'right to repair' and other related issues are beyond the scope of this rulemaking as they assume ownership of a copy. Such concerns (to the extent they legitimately exist) are best addressed within the context of the Office's examination of section 1201.").

[179] For example, there has been no shortage of public outcry about John Deere's practices with respect to their tractors. *See, e.g.*, Dan Nosowitz, *Farmers Demand Right to Right to Fix Their Own Dang Tractors*, MODERN FARMER (July 18, 2016), http://modernfarmer.com/2016/07/right-to-repair/; Laura Sydell, *DIY Tractor Repair Runs Afoul of Copyright Law*, NPR (Aug. 17, 2015), http://www.npr.org/sections/alltechconsidered/2015/08/17/432601480/diy-tractor-repair-runs-afoul-of-copyright-law. In addition, there have been efforts at the state level to enact "right to repair" statutes. Massachusetts enacted such a law in 2013, and similar legislation has been considered by other states. *See Legislation*, REPAIR.ORG, http://repair.org/legislation/. Automakers also have entered into a voluntary agreement allowing independent repair shops to more readily repair automobiles. *See* Gabe Nelson, *Automakers agree to 'right to repair' deal*, AUTOMOTIVE NEWS (Jan. 25, 2014), http://www.autonews.com/article/20140125/RETAIL05/301279936/automakers-agree-to-right-to-repair-deal. As the Copyright Office noted in its most recent 1201 rulemaking recommendation, however, this voluntary arrangement is limited in certain ways. 2015 SECTION 1201 RECOMMENDATION at 240 (noting that the agreement "does not apply to a significant portion of the vehicles that would be covered by the proposed exemption, including pre-2002 models and mechanized agricultural vehicles").

1.   Idea/Expression Dichotomy, Merger, and *Scènes à Faire*

The idea/expression dichotomy codified in section 102(b) of the Copyright Act preserves the ability of a repair technician or hobbyist to identify embedded software's underlying processes and methods of operation, replicate those methods using their own code, and add to those methods as necessary. It also preserves the ability to share those methods and techniques with other consumers, hobbyists, or technicians. Section 102(b) permits the use of those ideas described or embodied in software, so long as no lines of code are actually copied.

But even if a user borrows portions of code from an embedded program to effectuate a repair, for use in a replacement part, or to tinker with the product's existing capabilities, there are circumstances where those portions would not be eligible for copyright protection. As noted above in Part III.B, the merger and *scènes à faire* doctrines can play an important role. Thus, where there is one way or a limited number of ways to implement an idea, process, procedure, or method of operation, the merger doctrine may limit the scope of the copyright in that program. And where the expressive elements of the embedded program may be influenced by external factors, such as the mechanical specifications for the device or part, or relevant industry standards, the *scènes à faire* doctrine may likewise limit the scope of the copyright.

2.   *De Minimis* Uses

In cases where the idea/expression dichotomy and the doctrines of merger and *scènes à faire* do not apply, a consumer, repair technician, or software enthusiast may be able to copy, distribute, or display specific portions of an embedded program if the court determines that the user borrowed a *de minimis* portion of the code. A finding of *de minimis* infringement may be based on whether the user borrowed a relatively small amount of code when compared to the program as a whole. Alternatively, the finding could conceivably be based on whether the user borrowed portions of the code accounting for relatively minor features of the program, or portions controlling relatively mundane features of the software-enabled device.

Similarly, users may be able to modify the code for an embedded program if the court concludes that the modified version does not contain a sufficient amount of new material to qualify as a derivative work.[180] In such cases, the minor modification could be excused as a *de minimis* infringement of the copyright owner's right to create derivative works based on the original program.[181]

---

[180] *See generally* COMPENDIUM (THIRD) § 311.2.

[181] For example, one commenter noted that after Nest bought Revolv—a company making a smart hub used to control a home's devices such as lights, alarms, and doors—it shut down the cloud service to which the hub connected, essentially "shutting off" customers' homes. Tr. at 149:20-150:14 (May 24, 2016) (Kyle Wiens,

3.   Section 117

Sections 117(a) and (c) of the Copyright Act provide additional protection that may allow consumers, repair technicians, and software enthusiasts to fix or tinker with their software-enabled devices. Properly construed, section 117 "should adequately protect most repair and maintenance activities."[182]

As noted above, section 117(a) only applies to the "owner of a copy of a computer program."[183] Based on that limitation, some commenters were concerned that consumers cannot rely on section 117(a) because "they aren't considered owners" or because the exceptions "are simply too narrow."[184] As discussed above, however, many software-enabled products are sold without any license agreement, in which case a purchaser of that device should be considered the owner of both the device itself and the software embedded therein, and should be entitled to repair or maintain that program consistent with section 117(a).

In cases where these devices are sold with a written license agreement, the owner of the device may nevertheless be deemed to own both the device itself and the copy of the software embedded within that device. Again, the determination of whether the software copy is owned or licensed turns on the nature of the transaction between the parties. The *Vernor* and *Krause* decisions explain that a key part of the inquiry is whether the purchaser has the right to possess and use the product and its embedded software indefinitely and without restriction.[185] A licensing term prohibiting repair or tinkering would not, standing alone, compel the result that the software is licensed, rather than owned, for purposes of section 117; for instance, such a term would not itself "significantly restrict[] the user's ability to transfer the software" under the *Vernor* test.[186]

---

iFixit and Repair.org). According to this commenter, a consumer could repair his or her Revolv smart hub "without either rewiring the entire house and replacing all the devices" simply by "modify[ing] the [Revolv] firmware and [loading] some software that excludes the cloud check." Tr. at 150:15-19 (May 24, 2016) (Kyle Wiens, iFixit and Repair.org). It may be that these changes were sufficiently limited so as not to implicate the derivative work right.

[182] Auto Care Ass'n Initial Comments at 11; *see also* Tr. at 155:16-20 (May 18, 2016) (Aaron Perzanowski, Case Western Reserve University School of Law) ("If the standard for what counts as ownership is clarified and people can rely on 117, . . . that addresses many, although not all of the circumstances where we might otherwise be telling clients to focus their efforts on fair use.").

[183] 17 U.S.C. § 117(a).

[184] Tr. at 189:10-14 (May 24, 2016) (Erica Sollazzo, Engine Advocacy) ("[O]ne of the big problems right now is that consumers aren't able to take advantage of the limitations in . . . section 117 because they aren't considered owners."); iFixit Initial Comments at 8-9 ("The few carve-outs in the law are simply too narrow and do not effectively safeguard hardware repair for software-enabled devices.").

[185] *See Vernor*, 621 F.3d at 1111; *Krause*, 402 F.3d. at 124.

[186] *Vernor*, 621 F.3d at 1110.

In addition, when assessing the nature of the transaction with a consumer, it may also be appropriate to consider the software's relationship to the product being sold. For instance, in *Krause*, the court assessed whether substantial consideration was paid for the copy of the software at issue in that case.[187] Although that question can be complex in the context of embedded software,[188] it would be appropriate to focus on whether the software components of the product are ancillary or supplementary to non-software components of the product. For example, specialized software controlling certain mechanical components of an automobile, like windshield wipers or transmission, may essentially be invisible to the consumer. In such cases, it would be unusual to characterize the sale of the automobile as involving the licensing of that software for purposes of the Copyright Act. In contrast, it is very likely that a different result would obtain with respect to the operating system software in a personal computer, which— from the consumer's perspective—will be a more significant element of the transaction.

If the embedded software copy is owned, section 117(a) provides broad protections for repair and tinkering activities. As noted, that provision states that the owner of the copy of a computer program may make a new copy of that program or may create an adaptation of that program if the "new copy or adaptation is created as an essential step in the utilization of the computer program in conjunction with a machine," and "is used in no other manner."[189] It also states that the owner may authorize a third party—such as a repair technician—to make an additional copy or create an adaptation on his or her behalf.[190]

Accordingly, section 117(a) has been interpreted to permit a broad range of activities, including fixing bugs, transferring programs to a new operating system, and adding new features to make the software more useful to its owner.[191] Thus, the provision should allow the owner to make an "intermediate" copy of his or her program and transfer that copy into a test environment for the purpose of studying the code for errors

---

[187] *Krause*, 402 F.3d. at 124.

[188] *See* Copyright Alliance Initial Comments at 14 ("Today, more products are moving toward an approach that combines hardware with software to improve the functionality of traditional and newer product lines. Often, the software component is one of the most valuable aspects of the product.").

[189] 17 U.S.C. § 117(a).

[190] *Id.*

[191] *Krause*, 402 F.3d at 125 (finding that "correcting programming errors or 'bugs,' which interfered with the proper functioning of the programs" and "adaptation of the programs so that they would function on Titleserv's new Windows-based system," was protected under 117(a)); *id.* at 128 (finding that "modest alterations" such as adding features to improve the functionality of software for which it was created were protected under 117(a), and noting that the CONTU Report "specifically contemplate[d] protection for modifications adding features, rather than merely securing continued functioning of what was originally created").

that may prevent the program from working properly.[192] It also should enable the owner to make changes to the code that are necessary to ensure that the program functions properly, or to add features to improve the functionality of software for which it was created. Section 117(a) further should allow the owner to make an archival copy of the original program in case it is necessary to compare the source code for the original version and the adapted version.[193] Additionally, section 117(a) should allow the owner to transfer the copy of the original program or the adapted program (as the case may be) from the test environment back onto the software-enabled device, provided that the "intermediate" copy and any archival copies are deleted from the test environment. The provision also should enable the owner to transfer the original code or the adapted code (as the case may be) onto a replacement part that may be needed for the software-enabled device, provided that any "intermediate" and archival copies are deleted from the test environment, and provided that the original copy of the program is deleted from the part that has been replaced.[194] Most importantly, section 117(a) should allow the owner of the copy to authorize a third party to engage in any of these activities on his or her behalf, such as an independent repair technician.[195]

Section 117(c) covers a somewhat narrower range of activities. This provision principally was aimed at protecting independent repair technicians from copyright liability when they turned on a machine and made a reproduction of the software into RAM.[196] In the context of software-enabled products, this provision should allow the owner of a device (or his or her designee) to make a RAM copy of any programs that are stored within the device, and are necessary for the machine to be activated, to the extent that those copies are needed to service, repair, or restore that device "in order to make it work in accordance with its original specifications."[197] In addition, section 117(c) would shield the owner (or his or her designee) from infringement liability for making RAM copies to the extent that the owner may want to enhance the capabilities of his or her device, as the definitions of "maintenance" and "repair" in section 117(d) encompass

---

[192] *Cf.* 2015 SECTION 1201 RECOMMENDATION at 304-305 ("In order to understand the functionality of a computer program, one may need to make a copy to use it in conjunction with a 'machine,' such as a general-purpose computer, on which the program will be analyzed.").

[193] *See* 17 U.S.C. § 117(a)(2).

[194] *Aymes v. Bonnelli*, 47 F.3d 23, 26 (2d Cir. 1995) (internal citation omitted) (noting that "[t]his right of adaptation includes 'the right to add features to the program that were not present at the time of rightful acquisition,'" such as modifying an existing program to run on "successive generations" of hardware).

[195] 17 U.S.C. § 117(a)(2) (authorizing "the owner of a copy of a computer program to make or authorize the making of another copy or adaptation of that computer program" for archival purposes).

[196] *See* H.R. REP. NO. 105-551 at 27.

[197] 17 U.S.C. § 117(d)(1)-(2); *see also Storage Tech. Corp. v. Custom Hardware Eng'g & Consulting, Inc.*, 421 F.3d 1307, 1314 (Fed. Cir. 2005) (discussing these provisions).

servicing or restoring the machine to make it work "in accordance with . . . any *changes* to those specifications authorized for that machine."[198]

Although sections 117(a) and (c) may allow consumers, repair technicians, and software enthusiasts to fix or tinker with their software-enabled devices, section 117(b) places some limitations on the subsequent lease, sale, or transfer of copies made lawfully under section 117. While section 117(b) allows for "*exact* copies" made lawfully under section 117 to be "leased, sold, or otherwise transferred . . . only as part of the lease, sale, or other transfer of *all* rights in the program," *adaptations* so made may be "transferred only with the authorization of the copyright owner."[199] The first sale doctrine is "thus rendered totally inapplicable to the transfer of adaptations made pursuant to Section 117."[200] Accordingly, there may be limits on a consumer's ability to freely sell a device with modified embedded software.

4. Fair Use

A number of commenters stated that repairing or tinkering with a software-enabled consumer product should be considered a fair use under section 107,[201] though there also was concern about the uncertainty of the defense.[202]

The Copyright Office heard several suggestions for clarifying the scope of the fair use doctrine, such as: (1) requiring copyright owners to make a good faith determination that the defendant's conduct does not qualify as a fair use before filing suit;[203] (2) shifting

---

[198] 17 U.S.C. § 117(d)(1)-(2) (emphasis added).

[199] *Id.* § 117(b) (emphasis added).

[200] 2 NIMMER ON COPYRIGHT § 8.08[B][3].

[201] *See, e.g.*, Auto Care Ass'n Initial Comments at 11 ("Fair use also can assure that the scope of repair under patent law is not diminished by copyright law, and can fill gaps where the existing copyright statutory framework provides no explicit guidance."); Engine Advocacy Initial Comments at 13 ("Fair use also protects tinkering with or copying for the purpose of repairs or testing software embedded in devices. Making such uses is transformative and poses no risk of market substitution or harm to the underlying software work."); Tr. at 148:21-149:04 (May 24, 2016) (Ashley Ailsworth, SEMA) ("[I]f you are just interacting . . . with the parameters on the ECUs and not changing the really hardcore software and the firmware, . . . [t]here's a general understanding that that is a fair use . . . .").

[202] *See, e.g.*, Tr. at 149:13-18 (May 24, 2016) (Kyle Wiens, iFixit and Repair.org) ("[R]epair or modification of a vehicle that you own is a fair use . . . . And that's not the case now. That's not the perception in the market."); Tr. at 152:25-153:04 (May 24, 2016) (Kit Walsh, EFF) ("[T]he chilling effect both of 1201 but also on the expense and unpredictability of fair use . . . is manifested in the marketplace . . . people don't know if it's lawful under copyright to repair their car . . . ."); Tr. at 158:08-11 (May 18, 2016) (Shaun Bockert, Dorman Products, Inc.) ("We want to clarify that certain things qualify as non-infringing uses and we don't want to rely on just advising clients that this is probably a fair use . . . .").

[203] SEMA Initial Comments at 4 ("Another option would be to require a copyright owner to perform a subjective good faith analysis to determine whether the conduct at issue is for a purpose that constitutes fair use before . . . enforcing the DMCA's anti-circumvention provision.").

the burden of proof onto copyright owners to show a particular use was not fair;[204] (3) requiring a minimum threshold of commercial activity to sustain a finding of infringement;[205] or (4) increasing the availability of attorney's fees for prevailing defendants.[206] Others urged Congress or the Copyright Office to provide more specific guidance on fair use because it is so fact-specific,[207] expensive to litigate, difficult to communicate to a jury, and rarely presented until late in a judicial proceeding.[208]

The Copyright Office appreciates that fair use is a fact-intensive inquiry, and that the outcome of a particular lawsuit does not guarantee a similar outcome in cases involving other types of products. Although some suggested that Congress could address these concerns by adding "tinkering" or "repair" to the list of paradigmatic fair uses set forth in the preamble to section 107, such a change is not necessary. Even without a statutory amendment, the Office believes that, properly applied, the fair use factors—together with the existing case law—should ensure that consumers, repair technicians, and other interested parties will be able to engage in most traditional repair and tinkering activities without fear of copyright infringement liability. To assist courts and the public in applying the fair use doctrine, the Office offers the following generally applicable points regarding fair use analysis in the context of software-enabled everyday products. The Office cautions, however, that fair use analysis is ultimately a fact-specific inquiry, and the following analysis would not necessarily dictate the outcome of any particular case.

The first factor focuses on the purpose and character of the use, including whether the use is commercial in nature or for nonprofit educational purposes. To the extent that a repair is conducted by an individual for his or her own personal use, that activity would likely be considered a noncommercial use (albeit not a nonprofit educational use). Repairs conducted by a company or a technician engaged in the business of repairing embedded software or software-enabled devices would likely be considered a commercial use. But that does not necessarily mean that the repair is presumptively

---

[204] Tr. at 165:09-10 (May 24, 2016) (Cathy Gellis, Digital Age Defense) ("Right now, all the burdens seem to be on the fair user, and that's debilitating.").

[205] Tr. at 54:10-12 (May 24, 2016) (Kit Walsh, EFF).

[206] Auto Care Ass'n Initial Comments at 10.

[207] *See, e.g.,* Tr. at 157:18-25 (May 24, 2016) (Stephen Liu, Engine Advocacy) ("[T]he issue with fair use right now is that it's a defense and it's not very predictable. And the main reason for that is because every case is different. It's a fact-dependent analysis. The best way to resolve that, at least maybe the easiest way to resolve a lot of the problems that come from that is by creating carve-outs.").

[208] Tr. at 161:12-162:01 (May 24, 2016) (Cathy Gellis, Digital Age Defense) ("[F]air use is [assessed] way too late in the process . . . . How you even present that question to the jury is extremely problematic. It's massively expensive and very, very difficult to communicate."); Tr. at 171:23-172:11 (May 24, 2016) (Ashley Ailsworth, SEMA) ("[Fair use] case law is sufficiently clear actually. But the problem is . . . when you have companies, especially smaller companies that are having to operate in this space, and you really can't predict what a court's going to do and you never want to have to make that jump.").

ineligible for the fair use defense.[209] Instead, courts should also consider other aspects of the purpose and character of the use, as well as the three remaining factors.

In evaluating the purpose and character of the use, one important factor is that the fundamental purpose of any repair is to preserve or restore the functionality of a software-enabled device so that it may continue to be used. In this respect, repair supports—rather than displaces—the purpose of the embedded programs that control that device. Indeed, the Copyright Office made this same point in recommending in favor of an exemption for vehicle repair, diagnosis, and modification in the most-recent section 1201 rulemaking proceeding.[210]

In some cases, repair could be considered a "transformative" use under the first factor, because it often encourages the creation of new creative works. For instance, users may need to create diagnostic programs to study an embedded program and to identify potential issues with the code. If the problems are significant the user may need to modify or adapt the existing code. If those changes are sufficiently creative, the modified or adapted code may qualify as a new work based on the original version of the program.[211]

The second factor focuses on the nature of the copyrighted work. Courts and the Copyright Office have recognized that, in some instances, software may be entitled to less protection than other types of expressive works, such as music or films, because they are functional works.[212] In the repair context, the code for an embedded program is even further removed from traditionally expressive works. The user is typically interested in the portions of the code that are broken, rather than the portions that are capable of providing instructions to a software-enabled device. The fact that the program is damaged often means that it cannot be used for any purpose (expressive or otherwise). Even if the program contains both functioning and non-functioning elements, the user may need to transfer the entire program onto a test environment. Because embedded programs have no function when removed from a software-enabled device, the user may not be able to exploit the expressive elements of the program (if any) until the repair is complete.

---

[209] See Campbell v. Acuff-Rose Music, Inc., 510 U.S. 569, 584 (1994) (stating that "the commercial or nonprofit educational purpose of a work is only one element of the first factor enquiry into its purpose and character").

[210] 2015 SECTION 1201 RECOMMENDATION at 234-35 ("[T]he proposed uses for diagnosis and repair would presumably enhance the intended use of ECU computer programs.").

[211] See id. at 234 (noting that, in the context of automotive software, transformative uses "include copying the work to create new applications and/or tools that can interoperate with ECU software and facilitate functionalities such as diagnosis, modification and repair" or "modification of ECU computer programs to 'interoperate' with different auto parts").

[212] See, e.g., id. at 235 (noting "the Register's established position that computer programs such as those contained in ECUs are essentially functional works used to operate a device").

The third factor focuses on the amount and substantiality of the portion that has been used relative to the copyrighted work as a whole. The fact that a user may need to copy the entire program is not dispositive, particularly if the other factors weigh in favor of fair use. As the Copyright Office has elsewhere explained, "courts have been willing to permit extensive copying of the original work where it is necessary to accomplish a transformative purpose."[213] As mentioned above, such copying is often necessary to complete a repair: most computer programs do not have a specific beginning, middle, or end, which can make it difficult to identify the source of the problem within the code. Users often address this issue by making a copy of the entire program and transferring it onto a test environment. When the repair is complete, they typically transfer the program back onto the software-enabled device.

The fourth factor focuses on the effect on the potential market for or value of the copyrighted work. Repairing a software-enabled device is less likely to have an adverse impact on the potential market for the software embedded within that device. It is important in the context of software used to operate a particular device to focus on the market *for the relevant copyrighted work*—the software itself.[214] As discussed above, these types of computer programs are not distributed as standalone works. They are distributed with a specific device and their sole purpose is to operate or control that device. Because there is no market for the programs themselves and because the programs have no value apart from the devices that they operate, repairing these programs is not likely to interfere with any market likely exploited by the copyright owner. In the most recent section 1201 rulemaking, the Copyright Office made this same point in recommending the grant of an exemption for vehicle repair, diagnosis, and modification.[215] Although copyright owners may argue that repair activities effectively prevent them from offering authorized repair services for their own products, that is not the relevant issue: that market is not one that the copyright law was intended to protect.[216]

---

[213] *Id.* at 236.

[214] *See Lexmark*, 387 F.3d at 545.

[215] 2015 SECTION 1201 RECOMMENDATION at 236 (finding that, under the fourth fair-use factor, "[p]roponents have thus established that there is not a significant independent market for ECU computer programs that can be harmed").

[216] *See Lexmark*, 387 F.3d at 545 ("Lexmark's market for its toner cartridges and the profitability of its Prebate program may well be diminished by the SMARTEK chip, but that is not the sort of market or value that copyright law protects."); *Sony Comput. Entm't*, 203 F.3d at 607 ("Sony understandably seeks control over the market for devices that play games Sony produces or licenses. The copyright law, however, does not confer such a monopoly.").

C.   Security Research

Another area of inquiry was whether existing copyright law enables or frustrates the public's ability to engage in security research involving software-enabled consumer products. Researchers may study embedded software to identify potential flaws that may cause a device to malfunction or may allow the device to be compromised by third parties. In addition, academics as well as entities engaged in the business of conducting security research may want to share their discoveries with the public on a non-commercial basis.

Security research potentially implicates the following exclusive rights[217]:

- When studying an existing program for potential vulnerabilities, it is customary to make a copy of that program and transfer it into a test environment where it can be studied. This type of intermediate copying implicates the reproduction right under section 106(1).

- To correct a particular flaw the researcher may decide to change the existing code in some respect, add new code or remove existing lines of code, or develop new routines or entirely new programs that interoperate with the existing program. This type of activity potentially implicates the right to create derivative works under section 106(2). If the researcher decides to distribute copies of these derivative works, it may also implicate the distribution right under section 106(3).

- The researcher may decide to copy the program back onto the original device to determine if the patch was successful. This activity implicates the reproduction right under section 106(1).

- Often times, the researcher will publish his or her findings to alert the public about a flaw in a particular device. In some cases, the researcher may distribute an article or other written documentation that describes the problem and explains how to fix it. In other cases, the researcher may post his or her findings on a website or other public forum. If the researcher includes portions of the code for the embedded program, this may implicate the rights to reproduce, distribute, and publicly display that work under sections 106(1), 106(3), and 106(5). If the researcher includes any modifications that have been made to the program, it also may implicate the right to create derivative works under section 106(2).

---

[217] *See, e.g.,* Engine Advocacy Initial Comments at 11 (noting that security research "frequently requires that the software be copied first and then analyzed," which "may require copying, manipulation, or other engagement with the software").

Several commenters stated that these types of activities should be permitted because security research protects the general public against flaws in embedded software that could have dangerous consequences.[218] For example, "security researchers uncovered a loophole in the infotainment system of a Jeep Cherokee that allowed them to remotely disable its transmission and brakes."[219] This research "led Fiat Chrysler to issue an unprecedented recall for 1.4 million vehicles, mailing out USB drives with a patch for the vulnerable infotainment systems and blocking the attack on the Sprint network that connected its cars and trucks."[220]

While some manufacturers affirmatively test their own products and provide their customers with patches when appropriate, the Copyright Office learned that many manufacturers do not.[221] In such cases, it was urged that professional security researchers should be allowed "to audit and analyze the features of the device in order to detect these vulnerabilities," and, if necessary, share their findings with the government and the general public to "put pressure on the company" to address these flaws.[222]

The Office also was told that some software-enabled products are subject to license agreements that limit security research.[223] For instance, one public advocacy organization reported that the EULA for the Nest thermostat prohibits the user from "sharing the results of functional and performance tests" involving the product, without prior authorization from Nest.[224] Copyright owners were also said to discourage researchers from disclosing the results of their research by issuing DMCA take-down

---

[218] *See, e.g.*, Engine Advocacy Initial Comments at 2 ("[S]ecurity researchers should be able to explore and analyze the embedded software to detect . . . flaws, security vulnerabilities, [and] hidden privacy risks . . . ."); Tr. at 116:24-25, 117:01-07 (May 24, 2016) (Kit Walsh, EFF) (citing a study conducted by Hewlett-Packard finding vulnerabilities in "60 percent of the most common internet of things devices").

[219] Engine Advocacy Initial Comments at 2.

[220] Andy Greenberg & Kim Zetter, *How the Internet of Things Got Hacked*, WIRED (Dec. 28, 2015), http://www.wired.com/2015/12/2015-the-year-the-internet-of-things-got-hacked/. Engine Advocacy commented that similar problems were discovered through security research on a Tesla Model S, a Chevrolet Corvette, a BMW, and a Mercedes Benz. *See* Engine Advocacy Initial Comments at 11.

[221] *See, e.g.*, Tr. at 117:23-25, 118:01-12 (May 24, 2016) (Kit Walsh, EFF) (stating that "security is often not a sort of a high investment priority for people who are deploying internet of things devices").

[222] Tr. at 118:19-119:01, 119:06-10 (May 24, 2016) (Kit Walsh, EFF).

[223] *See, e.g.*, CDT Initial Comments at 4 ("[S]ome software licenses expressly prohibit customers from reverse engineering software code, even to look for or patch vulnerabilities in the code."); Engine Advocacy Initial Comments at 11 ("[T]hese activities may require copying, manipulation, or other engagement with the software that may be prohibited by the license under which it is distributed.").

[224] Tr. at 67:25, 68:01-05 (May 24, 2016) (Kit Walsh, EFF); *see End User License Agreement*, NEST, https://nest.com/legal/eula/ ("You may not release the results of any performance or functional evaluation of any of the Product Software to any third party without prior written approval of Nest Labs for each such release.").

notices or threatening infringement actions,[225] and it was asserted that even a potential legal challenge may effectively prevent researchers from conducting this type of work.[226] These commenters suggested that establishing a broad statutory exemption for security research or by clarifying the scope of the fair use doctrine would address these concerns.[227]

There are significant benefits to allowing security researchers to study software-enabled consumer products for potential vulnerabilities and to share their findings with the general public. In addition, as the Office has previously stated, rules governing security research "hardly seem the province of copyright, since the considerations of how safely to encourage such investigation are fairly far afield from copyright's core purpose of promoting the creation and dissemination of creative works."[228] In many cases, it may be more appropriate for these issues to be "considered by those responsible for our national security and for regulating the consumer products and services at issue."[229] Indeed, cybersecurity issues relating to software-enabled consumer products are being studied by other parts of the government, including the Department of Commerce's Internet Policy Task Force, which "is conducting a comprehensive review of the nexus between cybersecurity challenges in the commercial sector and innovation in the Internet economy."[230]

As will be discussed below, after reviewing the record, the Copyright Office does not see a need for legislative action with respect to the role of copyright law and security research at this time, for several reasons.[231] First, while there was some isolated evidence to suggest that software-enabled devices are subject to license agreements that would limit security research, as addressed in detail in Part IV.E below, it seems likely that the remedies for breach of such agreements would be found in state contract law, not copyright.[232]

---

[225] Tr. at 166:18-19 (May 18, 2016) (John Bergmayer, Public Knowledge); Tr. at 119:02-05 (May 24, 2016) (Kit Walsh, EFF); Aaron Perzanowski et al. Initial Comments at 7 ("Concerns about potential infringement liability can also discourage research and testing of consumer devices.").

[226] Tr. at 167:12-16 (May 18, 2016) (Aaron Perzanowski, Case Western Reserve University School of Law) ("[W]hile security researchers themselves might be willing to take risks, university general counsels are not known for being big risk takers. And their willingness to back researchers who are engaging in work that might draw litigation is rather limited.").

[227] Tr. at 164:06-08 (May 18, 2016) (John Bergmayer, Public Knowledge) (noting, in response to a question on fair use, "security research ought to categorically be non-infringing . . . [through] statute").

[228] 2015 SECTION 1201 RECOMMENDATION at 316.

[229] *Id.*

[230] *Cybersecurity*, U.S. DEP'T OF COMMERCE, https://www.ntia.doc.gov/category/cybersecurity.

[231] As noted, this study is not addressing the effects of section 1201, which are the topic of a separate study.

[232] The Copyright Office believes that the other components of the government, working together with industry, have an important role to play in encouraging and facilitating independent good faith security

In addition, the Office notes that industry practices regarding security research are rapidly developing. A growing number of copyright owners *encourage* users to conduct security research, and some companies even offer monetary incentives for those who identify problems and potential solutions. For example, Google has offered a "Vulnerability Reward Program" since 2010 to encourage security researchers to identify technical vulnerabilities in its system,[233] and it offers $500 to $100,000 for researchers who identify qualifying bugs through its "Chrome Reward Program."[234] Other companies such as Facebook,[235] Microsoft,[236] and Mozilla[237] offer similar security research rewards programs, while companies such as Oracle[238] and Apple[239] encourage security research without providing financial incentives.

Finally, a new statutory copyright framework for security research does not appear to be necessary, because—as addressed in detail below—existing copyright law doctrines, properly interpreted, should protect this legitimate activity from infringement liability.

1.   Idea/Expression Dichotomy, Merger, and *Scènes à Faire*

As discussed above in the context of tinkering and repair, section 102(b) of the Copyright Act gives researchers the ability to examine code for the purpose of studying its basic processes and methods of operation. Although this provision would not, in and of itself, shield a researcher from liability for making copies or derivative works in the course of their research, it would give researchers the ability to share these discoveries and insights with others.

But even where it may be necessary to copy, distribute, or display actual portions of the code, that does not necessarily mean that the researcher has violated the copyright

---

research. Tr. at 118:13-18, 119:06-10 (May 24, 2016) (Kit Walsh, EFF) (suggesting that government and public advocacy groups can play a constructive role in encouraging companies to disclose and remedy defects in their products).

[233] *Google Vulnerability Reward Program (VRP) Rules*, GOOGLE, https://www.google.com/about/appsecurity/reward-program/.

[234] *Chrome Reward Program Rules*, GOOGLE, https://www.google.com/about/appsecurity/chrome-rewards/.

[235] *Information*, FACEBOOK (May 11, 2016), https://www.facebook.com/whitehat.

[236] *Microsoft Bounty Programs*, MICROSOFT, https://technet.microsoft.com/en-us/library/dn425036.aspx.

[237] *Client Bug Bounty Program*, MOZILLA, https://www.mozilla.org/en-US/security/client-bug-bounty/. [238]

How to Report Security Vulnerabilities to Oracle, ORACLE, https://www.oracle.com/support/assurance/vulnerability-remediation/reporting-security-vulnerabilities.html. One commenter cited a blog post written by Oracle's chief security officer that discouraged third parties from conducting security research. CDT Initial Comments at 4 n.18. But Oracle reportedly removed the post from its website the day after it was published. *See* Sean Gallagher, *Oracle security chief to customers: Stop checking our code for vulnerabilities*, ARS TECHNICA (Aug. 11, 2015), http://arstechnica.com/information-technology/2015/08/oracle-security-chief-to-customers-stop-checking-our-code-for-vulnerabilities/.

[239] *Apple Web Server Notifications*, APPLE (July 11, 2016), https://support.apple.com/en-us/HT201536.

owner's exclusive rights. Where the vulnerability relates to purely functional code, the operation of which is dictated by external factors, or by the processes or algorithms the code embodies, copyright law would not prohibit the copying of that code, under the merger and *scènes à faire* doctrines, which are discussed in greater detail above.

2.   *De Minimis* Uses

Even where the idea/expression dichotomy, or the merger and *scènes à faire* doctrines do not apply, a security researcher copying protected expression from an embedded program may not be liable for copyright infringement if the court determines that the researcher only used a *de minimis* portion of the code.

For instance, if the researcher copied, distributed, or displayed a few (qualitatively unimportant) lines of code from a program containing thousands of routines, a court may conclude that the use was *de minimis* when compared to the program as a whole. The court may reach the same conclusion if the researcher only borrowed the flawed portions of the code that do not work at all, or the defective portions that undermine the basic functionality or integrity of the device. Likewise, if the researcher corrected these issues by modifying portions of the original code, the court may permit that use if it concludes that the modified version does not contain a sufficient amount of new material to qualify as a derivative work.

3.   Section 117

Sections 117(a) and (c) of the Copyright Act provide additional options that may allow security researchers to identify vulnerabilities in software-enabled devices, although these sections would not allow the researcher to share his or her findings with third parties without permission from the copyright owner.

As mentioned above, section 117(a) may be invoked by the "owner of a copy of a computer program," while section 117(c) may be invoked by "the owner or lessee of a machine . . . that lawfully contains an authorized copy of the computer program."[240] In many cases, the security researcher would likely be the owner of the device that he or she is studying. The researcher may also be considered the owner of any programs that are embedded within that device if it was sold without any license agreement. Moreover, in cases where the device was sold with a written license agreement, the researcher may be deemed to own both the device and the copy of the embedded software. As discussed in the repair and tinkering section above, that determination turns on the nature of the transaction between the manufacturer and the consumer, including the terms of the license.

---

[240] 17 U.S.C. § 117(a), (c).

As a preliminary matter, section 117(c) should allow a security researcher to make a RAM copy of any program stored within the device, to the extent that the program is needed to activate the device for the purpose of maintaining or repairing the machine to make it work "in accordance with its original specifications."[241] Likewise, the researcher should be able to make a RAM copy of any programs necessary for activation and stored within the device for the purpose of making the machine work "in accordance with . . . any changes to those specifications authorized for that machine."[242] This may be useful in cases where the researcher needs to modify a device's default specifications to identify errors in the code or to test potential fixes for the problem.

As noted in the context of tinkering and repair, section 117(a) has been interpreted to permit such activities as fixing bugs, transferring programs to a new operating system, and adding new features to make the software more useful to its owner.[243] Indeed, in the context of the section 1201 rulemaking, the Copyright Office has concluded that "reproduction and alteration of computer programs is often an 'essential step' in the process of identifying potential flaws."[244] Thus, section 117(a) should allow the researcher to engage in a broader range of activities (assuming he or she qualifies as an "owner" of a copy of the program). First, it should allow the researcher to make an "intermediate" copy and transfer that copy into a test environment for the purpose of identifying vulnerabilities in the code that may put that device at risk.[245] Second, it should allow the researcher to fix the problem by adding, removing, or modifying the code, as needed.[246] Third, it should allow the researcher to make an archival copy of the original program to compare the modified version of the program with the source code for the original version.[247] Fourth, it should allow the researcher to transfer the program (including any modifications that have been made) from the test environment onto the software-enabled device, provided that the researcher deletes any "intermediate" copies and archival copies from the test environment.[248] Fifth, section 117(a) should allow the

---

[241] 17 U.S.C. § 117(d)(1)-(2).

[242] *Id.*

[243] *Krause*, 402 F.3d at 125, 128-29 (finding that section 117(a) authorized owner to fix bugs, adapt program to work with a new operating system, and make "modest alterations" to add functionality).

[244] 2015 SECTION 1201 RECOMMENDATION at 304.

[245] *Id.* at 304-05 ("In order to understand the functionality of a computer program, one may need to make a copy to use it in conjunction with a 'machine,' such as a general-purpose computer, on which the program will be analyzed.").

[246] *Krause*, 402 F.3d at 125, 128.

[247] 2015 SECTION 1201 RECOMMENDATION at 305 ("[T]he creation of backup copies of computer programs may be important for security research—whether to serve as a baseline for comparison during experiments, or to restore a vehicle ECU to its original state after research is completed. These activities may well be covered by the provision permitting creation of archival-purpose copies, addressed in section 117(a)(2).").

[248] *Cf. Krause*, 402 F.3d at 126-29 (holding that the addition of new features was authorized under section 117(a)).

researcher to authorize a third party to conduct any of these activities on his or her behalf, such as a teaching assistant.[249]

That said, section 117(b) may impose some limitations on the researcher's ability to disseminate the results of his or her research. If the researcher modified the code for the original program, he or she would be allowed to share those modifications with third parties "only with the authorization of the copyright owner" of the original program.[250] While there is evidence to suggest that copyright owners actually encourage security researchers to study their code for potential flaws, and invite them to share their findings, to the extent that copyright owners withhold their consent, the researcher may have to rely on one of the other legal doctrines discussed in this section.

4.   Fair Use

Many commenters held the view that security research is clearly protected under the fair use doctrine,[251] although some expressed concern that this view is not widely shared among security researchers.[252] Indeed, there was significant concern about the lack of certainty that fair use alone would permit security researchers to pursue and disclose their work.[253] While it was noted that the Copyright Office's decisions in the 1201 rulemaking process may provide some guidance on these issues,[254] the Office was informed that stakeholders could not comfortably rely on the Office's conclusions regarding fair use in a litigation setting.[255] Proposals to address this concern included requiring a minimum threshold of commercial activity to sustain a finding of infringement.[256]

To be sure, there is little case law on the issue of whether security research constitutes fair use, and the reasoning in a section 1201 rulemaking proceeding does not guarantee a

---

[249] 17 U.S.C. § 117(a) (permitting the software copy owner to "make or authorize the making" of copies and adaptations).

[250] *Id.* § 117(b).

[251] *See, e.g.*, Tr. at 152:12-16 (May 24, 2016) (Kit Walsh, EFF) ("In the software context, . . . it's pretty clear that . . . security research is within the scope of what ultimately would be found to be a fair use by a court.").

[252] Tr. at 149:18-19 (May 24, 2016) (Kyle Wiens, iFixit and Repair.org); Tr. at 139:04-08 (May 18, 2016) (John Bergmayer, Public Knowledge) ("[W]e really do need to sort of have a robust understanding that security researchers[,] through whatever copyright doctrine, including fair use, are entitled to inspect software, to ensure that it is not putting people at risk.").

[253] Tr. at 152:15-21 (May 18, 2016) (Aaron Perzanowski, Case Western Reserve University School of Law).

[254] During the sixth triennial 1201 rulemaking, the Office concluded that the "overall record support[ed] proponents' claim that accessing and reproducing computer programs for purposes of facilitating good-faith security research and identification of defects are likely to be fair uses of the programs under section 107." 2015 SECTION 1201 RECOMMENDATION at 300.

[255] Tr. at 153:14-19 (May 18, 2016) (Aaron Perzanowski, Case Western Reserve University School of Law).

[256] Tr. at 54:10-12 (May 24, 2016) (Kit Walsh, EFF).

similar outcome in an actual litigated dispute involving security research. Nevertheless, the Copyright Office believes that, if properly applied, the four factors set forth in section 107, together with the existing case law in analogous areas, will likely ensure that legitimate security researchers will be able to engage in traditional, good-faith research activities without fear of liability. Although the determination of whether a particular use is fair ultimately depends on a fact-specific inquiry, the Office offers the following generally applicable points on how the factors may be applied in this context.

As an initial matter, the preamble to section 107 mentions "criticism," "comment," "news reporting," "scholarship," and "research" as examples of activities that are traditionally considered to be fair use.[257] These terms are likely broad enough to cover the types of activities that are traditionally associated with good-faith security research.[258]

The first factor focuses on the purpose and character of the use, including whether the use is commercial in nature or for nonprofit educational purposes. Security research is often conducted by academics, and in that context, it would likely be considered a noncommercial use. Research conducted by a company or an individual engaged in the business of security testing would likely be considered a commercial use. But it does not necessarily follow that the researcher would be ineligible for the fair use defense.[259] Again, courts would have to evaluate the other aspects of the purpose and character of the use and the three other fair use factors.

The primary purpose of any security research is to study an existing program to identify flaws in the code, and to share that information with users who may be adversely affected by those defects. This type of activity may result in comment or criticism about the program itself or the device that it operates. If the researcher shares his or her discoveries with the public, it also could be considered a form of news reporting. In some cases, the researcher may include portions of the actual code in his or her research, but the researcher may not be using those portions for the same purpose as the copyright owner. In other words, the researcher may not be using the code within a computing environment to control the operation of a software-enabled device. Instead, the researcher may be using the code as factual evidence of the errors that he or she discovered. And the researcher may be using those excerpts in an entirely different context, such as an article, blog post, or other written document that explains the nature

---

[257] 17 U.S.C. § 107.

[258] The Office reached a similar conclusion during the sixth triennial rulemaking. 2015 SECTION 1201 RECOMMENDATION at 300 ("[G]ood-faith security research encompasses several of the favored activities listed in the preamble of section 107.").

[259] *Campbell*, 510 U.S. at 584 ("If . . . commerciality carried presumptive force against a finding of fairness, the presumption would swallow nearly all of the illustrative uses listed in the preamble paragraph of § 107, including . . . research . . . .").

or the defect and the proposed solution. Fair use is likely to protect publication of research findings, including the relevant code.[260]

Another important purpose of security research is to eliminate the flaws in the code that may prevent the device from performing its intended function. In this respect, security research supports the purpose of the embedded programs that control that device. Security research could also be considered a "transformative" use under the first factor, because it often results in the creation of new creative works. For example, researchers may need to create diagnostic routines to identify the errors in an embedded program. To correct these errors the researcher may decide to modify or adapt the existing code, and if those changes are sufficiently creative, they may qualify as a new work of authorship.[261] Researchers may also publish articles describing their findings, or use their findings as the basis for other research.

The second factor focuses on the nature of the copyrighted work. As mentioned above, software may be entitled to less protection than other types of expressive works, because it is primarily functional in nature.[262] In the context of security research, the researcher often focuses on the defective lines of code, rather than the code that is actually capable of controlling or operating the software-enabled device. As a result, the code is even further removed from traditionally expressive works.

As discussed above, the third factor focuses on the amount and substantiality of the portion that has been used relative to the copyrighted work as a whole. The fact that a researcher may need to copy the entire program is not dispositive, particularly if the other factors weigh in favor of fair use. As the Copyright Office noted during the sixth triennial 1201 rulemaking, "where functional elements of a computer program cannot be investigated or assessed without some intermediate reproduction of the works, courts have held that the third factor is not of significant weight,"[263] and in such cases, the Office noted that the weight assigned to third factor "is slight."[264]

---

[260] *Id.* at 300 (noting that security research is likely to be a transformative use, because the "purpose of the use is to engage in academic inquiry" and "may result in criticism or comment about the work and the devices in which it is incorporated, including potential flaws and vulnerabilities").

[261] *See* 2015 SECTION 1201 RECOMMENDATION at 234 (noting that, in the context of automotive software, transformative uses "include copying the work to create new applications and/or tools that can interoperate with ECU software and facilitate functionalities such as diagnosis, modification and repair" or "modification of ECU computer programs to 'interoperate' with different auto parts").

[262] *See Oracle Am., Inc.,* 750 F.3d at 1375 ("[W]here the nature of the work is such that purely functional elements exist in the work and it is necessary to copy the expressive elements in order to perform those functions, consideration of this second factor arguably supports a finding that the use is fair."); *see also* 2015 SECTION 1201 RECOMMENDATION at 301 ("When a computer program is being used to operate a device, the work is likely to be largely functional in nature.").

[263] 2015 SECTION 1201 RECOMMENDATION at 301.

[264] *Id.*

The fourth factor focuses on the effect on the potential market for or value of the copyrighted work. Conducting security research on an embedded program is not likely to have an adverse impact on the potential market for that program, since it does not exist separately from the device. As with tinkering and repair, it is important to focus on the market *for the relevant copyrighted work.* In this case the relevant work is the embedded program itself, rather than discrete "bug fixes" that may be needed to correct the errors within that program.[265]

As discussed above, these programs are distributed with a specific device and often their sole purpose is to control that device. Security research is not likely to interfere with any market that the copyright owner is likely to exploit, because there is no market for the programs themselves, and they have no value apart from the device they operate. Moreover, security research is intended to prolong the useful life of these devices, rather than replacing them with a new program or a new device. Some commenters suggested that copyright owners may want to quash security research[266] as it may damage their reputation and the goodwill of their products. Reputational harm, however, is not the type of injury that the copyright law is intended to prevent, and so is irrelevant to the fair use analysis.[267]

D.   *Interoperability and Competition*

Another subject of the Committee's request is the examination of whether, and the extent to which, "the design, distribution, and legitimate uses of products" and "innovative services" are "being enabled and/or frustrated by the application of copyright law to software in everyday products."[268] The Copyright Office's inquiry focused on whether the copyright law furthers or hinders development of interoperable products and services and competition in the area of software-enabled consumer products.

The development of interoperable products and services may implicate a number of the exclusive rights set forth under section 106 of the Copyright Act:

- Section 106(1)'s reproduction right is implicated when intermediate copies of a program are made and transferred for purposes of "reverse engineering" the

---

[265] *See Lexmark,* 387 F.3d at 545; *Sony Comput. Entm't,* 203 F.3d at 607.

[266] *See, e.g.,* Tr. at 118:19-119:04 (May 24, 2016) (Kit Walsh, EFF) ("You heard from a whole bunch of security researchers about the need for members of the public, without permission, to be able to audit and analyze the features of the device in order to detect these vulnerabilities and put pressure on the company. . . . Sometimes the company will respond by threatening you, trying to silence your disclosure of that research using copyright law or DMCA . . . .").

[267] *See, e.g., Campbell,* 510 U.S. at 591-92 (noting that, like a parody, a scathing review "does not produce a harm cognizable under the Copyright Act").

[268] Grassley/Leahy Letter at 2.

program to determine compatibility requirements, and may be implicated when pieces of code needed to enable interoperability are copied from the original program into other software or devices.

- Section 106(2)'s right to prepare derivative works potentially is implicated by modification of the code on the product to facilitate interoperability, or development of new programs that interoperate with the existing program.

- Section 106(3)'s distribution right is implicated when the new software, device, or replacement part is transferred to a third party.

Commenters raised concerns about whether current law contains adequate safeguards to enable interoperability and preserve competition. For example, there may be challenges in applying somewhat indeterminate doctrines such as fair use to software, and while the Copyright Act includes various doctrines to address these concerns, "in the software world, they continue to be litigated and re-litigated, keeping them in legal limbo."[269] To remedy this situation, some urged legislation to "clarify that companies cannot use copyright law coupled with lockout codes to restrict competition in replacement parts."[270] At the same time, the Copyright Office heard that the current law already effectively enables interoperability and competition through the application of existing exceptions and limitations, and that no statutory changes are presently needed.[271]

The Copyright Office recognizes the importance of preserving the ability to develop products and services that can interoperate with software-enabled consumer products, and the goal of preserving competition in the marketplace.[272] At this time, however, the Office believes that statutory change is not warranted. First, while a new statutory framework might initially help reduce some uncertainty in this area, the risk is that any framework will become outdated in light of the rapid pace of technological development. Second, as even some public advocacy organizations suggested, faithful application of existing copyright law doctrines can preserve the twin principles of interoperability and competition.[273]

---

[269] Consumers Union Reply Comments at 4.

[270] Static Control Components Initial Comments at 2.

[271] ESA Initial Comments at 8 (urging that "[s]oftware is also subject to the generally-applicable limitations on the scope of copyright protection" and that "these limitations have proven flexible enough to accommodate innovation through development of products interoperable with those containing embedded software").

[272] *See* 2015 SECTION 1201 RECOMMENDATION 163 (noting that "interoperability is favored under the law").

[273] *See* Tr. at 42:17-43:03 (May 18, 2016) (John Bergmayer, Public Knowledge) ("I think there are existing copyright law doctrines that have been around for a really long time that . . . could already apply to at least prevent the use of copyright to limit competition by people making other competing products.");

1.   Idea/Expression Dichotomy, Merger and *Scènes à Faire*

Section 102(b) of the Copyright Act ensures that the ideas, processes, or methods of operation *embodied or described* in computer code cannot be protected by copyright. As a result, the Act does not prevent a competitor from studying code to determine the underlying methods it teaches, and from implementing those methods using *different* code than the original, to create an interoperable or competitive software-enabled consumer product.[274]

Indeed, "clean room" implementations using exactly this process have long been used by the computer hardware and software industries to ensure development of competitive products. One famous example of this involves Phoenix Technologies, which wanted to produce a new BIOS for personal computers that was compatible with the BIOS produced by the dominant market player, IBM. To achieve that objective, Phoenix engineers "studied the IBM BIOS—about 8KB of code—and described everything it did as completely as possible without using or referencing any actual code."[275] Then, "Phoenix brought in a second team of programmers who had no prior knowledge of the IBM BIOS and had never seen its code" and "[w]orking only from the first team's functional specifications . . . wrote a new BIOS that operated as specified."[276] "The resulting Phoenix BIOS was different from the IBM code, but for all intents and purposes, it operated identically."[277] As a result, "Phoenix began selling its BIOS to companies that then used it to create the first IBM-compatible PCs."[278] As this example demonstrates, section 102(b) has served a critical function in preserving competition.

Even though computer code is considered expression, that expression still may be copied if it is subject to the limiting doctrines of merger or *scènes à faire*. These doctrines are a promising avenue to permit copying for purposes of interoperability, at least in the narrow circumstances in which they may apply. As noted, merger and *scènes à faire*

Consumers Union Reply Comments at 4 (noting that "in an ideal world, these clarifications might be accomplished in the courts").

[274] Several commenters urged that if a portion of computer code—such as an application programming interface, or API—is essential to achieve interoperability, that portion is unprotectable as a "system" or "method of operation" within the meaning of section 102(b). *See, e.g.,* Aaron Perzanowski et al. Initial Comments at 8-9; CDT Initial Comments at 1-2 (suggesting this area of law is "unclear"); EFF Initial Comments at 9-10; Engine Advocacy Initial Comments at 5-8. The U.S. government, however, has expressly taken a contrary view in litigation before the Supreme Court. Brief for the United States as Amicus Curiae at 15-16, *Google, Inc. v. Oracle Am., Inc.,* 135 S. Ct. 2887 (2016) (No. 14-410), 2015 WL 2457656. This study does not provide the occasion to reconsider that position.

[275] Matthew Schwartz, *Reverse-Engineering,* Computerworld (Nov. 12, 2001), http://www.computerworld.com/article/2585652/app-development/reverse-engineering.html.

[276] *Id.*

[277] *Id.*

[278] *Id.*

appear to be especially relevant to the sorts of software-enabled consumer products discussed in Part II above. In such products, software may be constrained by the mechanical or functional requirements of the product. For instance, software used to operate car windshield wipers may be dictated by fairly constrained specifications on how such wipers are supposed to work. In such cases, the merger and *scènes à faire* doctrines will ensure that copyright law does not prevent a competitor from making identical software based on those same constraints.

2. Fair Use

Courts repeatedly have used the fair use doctrine to permit copying necessary to enable the creation of interoperable software and products.[279] *Sega Enterprises v. Accolade, Inc.* and *Sony Computer Entertainment v. Connectix* are two of the leading cases addressing the issue of fair use for purposes of interoperability. In *Sega*, the Ninth Circuit found that a competitor in the video game market, who copied Sega's software to reverse-engineer the code and determine how to make its own game cartridges interoperable with Sega's console, was engaged in fair use.[280] The court considered such use to be transformative because the copying was done to create new works—video games—that interoperated with existing works.[281]

Similarly, in *Sony v. Connectix*,[282] the Ninth Circuit found that the making of intermediate copies of the PlayStation video game console's operating system to create a console emulator that did not duplicate the copyrighted code in the new work, but allowed a PC to play console games, was a fair use.[283] As in *Sega*, the court emphasized that the purpose of this reverse engineering was to create a new creative work—in this case, a gaming platform "that would be compatible with games designed for the Sony PlayStation."[284]

---

[279] *See, e.g., Atari Games Corp. v. Nintendo of Am. Inc.*, 975 F.2d 832, 842-44 (Fed. Cir. 1992) (holding that reverse engineering of a competitor's computer chips to "learn their unprotected ideas and processes" was a fair use).

[280] *Sega Enters. Ltd.*, 977 F.2d at 1514-15, 1520. *Sega* is considered a seminal case on fair use and interoperability of computer programs. *See, e.g.*, Aaron Perzanowski at 2; Auto Care Ass'n at 5; SEMA Initial Comments at 2. *Sega* was crucial for Congress in creating a reverse-engineering exception to anticircumvention rule in section 1201, 17 U.S.C. § 1201(f), as Congress specifically highlighted *Sega* in explaining that it did not want to hinder interoperability. *See* STAFF OF H. COMM. ON THE JUDICIARY, 105TH CONG., SECTION-BY-SECTION ANALYSIS OF H.R. 2281 AS PASSED BY THE UNITED STATES HOUSE OF REPRESENTATIVES ON AUGUST 4, 1998, at 14 (Comm. Print 1998).

[281] *Sega Enters. Ltd.*, 977 F.2d 1510, 1523 (9th Cir. 1992); *see also Sony Comput. Entm't*, 203 F.3d at 599-600.

[282] 203 F.3d 596 (9th Cir. 2000).

[283] *Sony Comput. Entm't*, 203 F.3d at 599, 602-08.

[284] *Id.* at 606-07.

Although not a case ultimately decided on fair use grounds, *Lexmark International, Inc. v. Static Control Components, Inc.*, discussed above, also offers some helpful guidance on fair use, particularly as it involved a competitor copying the relevant code into its own product. [285] The district court in *Lexmark* concluded that the fair use defense did not apply.[286] On appeal, the Sixth Circuit criticized two aspects of the district court's decision. First, with respect to the first fair use factor—the purpose of the use—the Sixth Circuit concluded that it was "far from clear that [the defendant] copied the Toner Loading Program for its commercial value *as a copyrighted work*."[287] Instead, the defendant was not "seeking to exploit or unjustly benefit from any creative energy that Lexmark devoted to writing the program code," but simply "to permit printer functionality."[288] Second, with respect to the fourth factor—the effect of the use on the value of the copyrighted material—the Sixth Circuit regarded the relevant question as being "whether the infringement impacted the market for the copyrighted work itself" rather than the product in which it was embedded.[289] The court found that Lexmark had failed to "introduce[] any evidence showing that an independent market exists for a program as elementary as its Toner Loading Program."[290]

The Copyright Office also has addressed fair use in the context of software-enabled consumer products during the section 1201 triennial rulemaking proceedings. For instance, the Office has in several prior rulemakings recommended adoption of an exemption to allow the "jailbreaking" of devices like smartphones, so that such devices can interoperate with a wide variety of third-party software applications, on the ground that such uses are likely to be fair.[291]

Based on the case law and the Office's prior statements, many commenters asserted that the fair use doctrine is working well to enable the creation of interoperable products, software, and services.[292] As other commenters noted, however, fair use is a highly fact-specific inquiry,[293] and thus a conclusive determination that a particular use is fair can

---

[285] *Lexmark Int'l, Inc.*, 387 F.3d at 544.

[286] *Lexmark Int'l, Inc. v. Static Control Components, Inc.*, 253 F. Supp. 2d 943, 960-62 (E.D. Ky. 2003).

[287] *Lexmark Int'l, Inc.*, 387 F.3d at 544.

[288] *Id.*

[289] *Id.*

[290] *Id.* at 545.

[291] *See* 2015 SECTION 1201 RECOMMENDATION 188-92.

[292] Tr. at 171:23-172:04 (May 24, 2016) (Ashley Ailsworth, SEMA) (stating that "the case law is sufficiently clear"); Tr. at 135:21-136:01 (May 18, 2016) (Jonathan Zuck, ACT) ("[F]air use, to the limited degree we have data at this point about its use in embedded devices, has been effective."); Tr. at 173:21-22 (May 24, 2016) (Kit Walsh, EFF) ("[F]or the most part we feel that the cases are pretty good.").

[293] Tr. at 135:10-12 (May 18, 2016) (Jonathan Zuck, ACT); Tr. at 168:16-18 (May 18, 2016) (Keith Kupferschmid, Copyright Alliance) ("[W]henever you talk about fair use, it's very, very context-specific, fact-specific. And we have to be very, very cautious if we move in any particular direction in that area.").

only come after litigation, which can make the fair use defense too expensive, unpredictable, or risky to rely on.[294] Some commenters called fair use "a fallback doctrine"[295] or a defense of last resort.[296] One commenter said this uncertainty in fair use law is chilling innovation and competition.[297] Some even suggested that the law surrounding fair use in the context of software-enabled everyday products is not more developed because of the fear of separate liability under section 1201 of the Copyright Act for circumventing technological protection measures.[298]

The Copyright Office also received suggestions for statutory changes regarding interoperability. Some commenters noted that the preamble for the Copyright Act's fair use provision includes paradigmatic examples—"criticism, comment, news reporting, teaching . . . scholarship, or research"[299]—that do not fit neatly into the software context, and suggested that new language addressing interoperability should be inserted into the fair use preamble.[300] Other commenters suggested that the Copyright Act should include a specific statutory carve-out, outside of the section 107 fair use defense, permitting copying of software for purposes of enabling interoperability,[301] or an interoperability exception that parallels the reverse-engineering exception in section 1201(f).[302] At the same time, commenters urged that any statutory carve-out should operate as "a floor on permitted activity rather than a ceiling."[303]

---

[294] Tr. at 56:17-19 (Kit Walsh, EFF) (May 24, 2016) ("Fair use is a very important catchall measure. But it can't be the first line of defense for people."); Tr. at 171:23-172:11 (May 24, 2016) (Ashley Ailsworth, SEMA) (case law is "sufficiently clear," but there is a risk that a court does not find fair use); Tr. at 158:03-14 (May 18, 2016) (Shaun J. Bockert, Dorman Products, Inc.) (fair use is not sufficiently clear to advise clients that reverse engineering of software is permitted).

[295] Tr. at 138:04-05 (May 18, 2016) (John Bergmayer, Public Knowledge).

[296] Tr. at 140:11-12 (May 18, 2016) (Shaun J. Bockert, Dorman Products, Inc.); Tr. at 155:14-15 (May 18, 2016) (Aaron Perzanowski, Case Western Reserve University School of Law).

[297] Tr. at 147:08-12 (May 24, 2016) (Kyle Wiens, iFixit) ("We have seen very little innovation around farm equipment in the United States, even though there's a huge amount of interest, because of . . . locked down interfaces and the fear that people have [of violating copyright law]."); see also Tr. at 148:06-11 (May 24, 2016) (Kyle Wiens, iFixit and Repair.org).

[298] Tr. at 152:12-18 (May 24, 2016) (Kit Walsh, EFF) ("[I]t's pretty clear that research for interoperability . . . is within the scope of what ultimately would be found to be a fair use by a court," but "[t]here are places where that case law hasn't . . . develop[ed] in large part because [technological protection measures] are chilling people.").

[299] 17 U.S.C. § 107.

[300] Tr. at 160:11-161:03 (May 24, 2016) (Stephen Liu, Engine Advocacy); Tr. at 170:20-25 (May 24, 2016) (Ashley Ailsworth, SEMA).

[301] Tr. at 28:7-17 (May 18, 2016) (Shaun J. Bockert, Dorman Products, Inc.).

[302] Tr. at 171:14-16 (May 24, 2016) (Ashley Ailsworth, SEMA).

[303] Tr. at 56:24-57:01 (May 24, 2016) (Kit Walsh, EFF).

Given the current state of the law, the Copyright Office does not believe that a specific statutory exemption permitting use of embedded software for purposes of enabling interoperability is necessary.[304] The case law generally holds that intermediate copying for purposes of reverse engineering and creation of interoperable software is, in most cases, a fair use.[305] Moreover, the Office believes that, in many cases, copying of appropriately limited amounts of code from one software-enabled product into a competitive one for purposes of compatibility and interoperability should also be found to be a fair use.[306]

To be sure, the Copyright Office appreciates the concerns raised by commenters regarding the uncertainty and fact-bound nature of the fair use doctrine. But fair use also has the benefit of being a flexible doctrine that can be used in a wide-variety of circumstances. Although Congress could address some of the concerns regarding the uncertain application of the fair use doctrine by adding the purpose of "enabling interoperability" to the list of paradigmatic fair uses in section 107 of the Copyright Act, the Office believes that such a change is not necessary at this time because existing law provides sufficient flexibility to protect interoperability.

Again, although fair use is ultimately a fact-specific inquiry, some general points can be made regarding the fair use analysis in this context. In assessing "the purpose and character of the use," the commercial nature of the use is not a bar to a finding of fair use.[307] Instead, in this context, it is more important to focus on whether the use is principally for the purpose of exploiting the creativity of the original author of the code,[308] or for some purpose "unrelated to copyright protection."[309] Under this analysis, intermediate copying for the purpose of studying the methods and functioning of code,

---

[304] Were Congress to create a specific statutory exception to enable interoperability, the Copyright Office would caution against using section 1201(f) as a model. As the Office has explained in the context of a section 1201 rulemaking, the "apparent purpose of [section 1201(f)] does not appear precisely to match its language." U.S. COPYRIGHT OFFICE, U.S. COPYRIGHT OFFICE, SECTION 1201 RULEMAKING: FIFTH TRIENNIAL PROCEEDING TO DETERMINE EXEMPTIONS TO THE PROHIBITION ON CIRCUMVENTION, RECOMMENDATION OF THE REGISTER OF COPYRIGHT 71 (2012) ("2012 SECTION 1201 RECOMMENDATION").

[305] See, e.g., Sony Comput. Entm't, 203 F.3d at 609; Sega Enters. Ltd., 977 F.2d at 1514, 1520; Atari Games Corp., 975 F.2d at 842-44; see also 2015 SECTION 1201 RECOMMENDATION at 188 (stating in the context of granting a jailbreaking exemption "allow[ing] [a] operating system on a device to interoperate with other programs [is] a favored purpose under the law.").

[306] Cf. Lexmark Int'l, Inc., 387 F.3d at 545-46.

[307] Campbell, 510 U.S. at 584 (holding that the commercial nature of a work is alone not dispositive of fair use, but an interest to balance); Sega Enters., 977 F.2d at 1522 (finding fair use and noting "the use at issue was an intermediate one only and thus any commercial 'exploitation' was indirect or derivative").

[308] As one commenter suggested, if the code at issue is a "distinguishing characteristic" of a product and that software "gives it a competitive advantage," then a second-comer's copying of that software for a competing product may be a factor cutting against fair use. Tr. at 36:18-22 (May 18, 2016) (Steve Tepp, GIPC).

[309] Lexmark Int'l, Inc., 387 F.3d at 544; Sega Enters., 977 F.2d at 1522-23 (noting that "Accolade copied Sega's code for a legitimate, essentially non-exploitative purpose").

so that those methods and functions can be embodied in new code, is likely to be a favored purpose.[310] And in some cases, even literal copying of code may be favored, if the purpose is simply to "permit . . . functionality" of a software-enabled device, and not to exploit the creativity of the original author.[311] Indeed, as the Copyright Office repeatedly has recognized, interoperability is "a favored purpose" under the first fair use factor.[312]

Courts also favor software interoperability when considering the second fair use factor, which concerns "the nature of the copyrighted work."[313] As noted above, works that are functional—like software embedded in and critical to the functioning of a consumer product—are entitled to lesser protection under the Copyright Act.[314]

The "amount and substantiality of the portion used" in many cases is likely to weigh against a finding of fair use, since it is often necessary to copy significant portions of the code to engage in reverse engineering activities. But this factor is also unlikely to be of significant relevance, where the other factors point in favor of fair use. [315]

Regarding the effect on the market or potential market for or value of the work, as already noted, it is important to focus on the market *for copyrighted works*.[316] For most software-enabled consumer products like those mentioned in Part II, there will not be a market for the software separate and apart from the consumer product. In such cases, the fourth factor is likely to favor fair use.[317] In the context of software-enabled

---

[310] *Sony Comput. Entm't,* 203 F.3d at 606-07; *Sega Enters.,* 977 F.2d at 1522.

[311] *Lexmark Int'l, Inc.,* 387 F.3d at 544.

[312] *See, e.g.,* 2015 SECTION 1201 RECOMMENDATION at 162, 163, 188; 2012 SECTION 1201 RECOMMENDATION at 163 (2012).

[313] 17 U.S.C. § 107(2).

[314] *Sega Enters.,* 977 F.2d at 1524; *Sony Comput. Entm't,* 203 F.3d at 603; 2015 SECTION 1201 RECOMMENDATION at 188.

[315] *See, e.g., Sony Comput. Entm't,* 203 F.3d at 606 ("[I]n a case of intermediate infringement when the final product does not itself contain infringing material, this factor is of 'very little weight.'" (quoting *Sega Enters.,* 977 F.2d at 1526-27)); 2015 SECTION 1201 RECOMMENDATION at 188-89 ("[W]hile jailbreaking often requires making a complete reproduction of the firmware, in light of the *de minimis* nature of the modifications ultimately made to the firmware to enable jailbreaking, this factor, while not favorable to fair use, is of limited relevance.").

[316] *See Lexmark Int'l, Inc.,* 387 F.3d at 544-45.

[317] Where, however, software provides a secure platform for other copyrighted works for which there is such a market, courts should examine carefully the impact on that market. *See, e.g.,* 2015 SECTION 1201 RECOMMENDATION at 199-200 (discussing video game console firmware); *id.* at 214-15 (discussing smart TV firmware).

consumer products in particular, the fourth factor also is likely to favor fair use where the purpose of the use is to create a "legitimate competitor in the market."[318]

As noted above, proper application of these principles should ensure that copyright law preserves the ability to create interoperable products and services.[319]

3.   Misuse

A number of commenters pointed to the equitable doctrine of "copyright misuse" as a potential means of ensuring that copyright protection for embedded software is not used for purely anticompetitive ends.[320] Copyright misuse is relatively unexamined among copyright defenses. It is a common law defense that initially developed in the context of overly restrictive licensing terms, that has "outgrown such antitrust like roots and now applies, *inter alia*, to efforts to misrepresent or extend rights beyond the scope of one's copyright."[321]

The leading case addressing the copyright misuse defense is the Fourth Circuit's decision in *Lasercomb America, Inc. v. Reynolds*.[322] There, the plaintiff included license terms for computer-aided design software preventing any licensee from making a competing software product.[323] The Fourth Circuit found that the plaintiff had misused the copyright, and barred the plaintiff from bringing an infringement action. The court noted that, while "much uncertainty engulfs the 'misuse of copyright' defense," at its core it prevents a copyright owner from "us[ing] its copyright in a particular expression . . . to control competition in an area outside the copyright."[324] Importantly, the court emphasized that "a misuse need not be a violation of antitrust law in order to comprise an equitable defense to an infringement action."[325]

Another illustrative case is *DSC Communications Corp. v. DGI Technologies, Inc.*, in which the manufacturer of a phone switching system, which utilized microprocessor cards containing copyrighted software, licensed those cards to customers with a restriction on

---

[318] *Sony Comput. Entm't*, 203 F.3d at 607; *cf. Sega Enters.*, 977 F.2d at 1523 ("Accolade did not attempt to 'scoop' Sega's release of any particular game or games, but sought only to become a legitimate competitor in the field of Genesis-compatible video games.").

[319] *Sega Enters.*, 977 F.2d at 1523-24 ("[A]n attempt to monopolize the market by making it impossible for others to compete runs counter to the statutory purpose of promoting creative expression and cannot constitute a strong equitable basis for resisting the invocation of the fair use doctrine.").

[320] *See, e.g.*, CCIA Initial Comments at 3-4 ("A more robust doctrine of copyright misuse would alleviate pressures arising from the improper assertion of rights.").

[321] 5 WILLIAM F. PATRY, PATRY ON COPYRIGHT § 17:128 (2016).

[322] 911 F.2d 970 (4th Cir. 1990).

[323] *Id.* at 972-73.

[324] *Id.* at 973, 979.

[325] *Id.* at 978.

copying the software for any purpose.[326] A competitor wanted to create competing, interoperable microprocessor cards despite the restriction.[327] Reviewing the scope of a preliminary injunction, the Fifth Circuit found the misuse defense would likely be successful, as the plaintiff appeared to be "attempting to use its copyright to obtain a patent-like monopoly over unpatented microprocessor cards."[328] The court reasoned that if the plaintiff were allowed to prevent copying in this manner, "then it can prevent anyone from developing a competing microprocessor card, even though it has not patented the card."[329]

Cases like *Lasercomb* and *DSC Communications*, as well as others outside the software context,[330] pave a path for a misuse defense to prevent anticompetitive behavior regarding copyright in embedded software. While there has been some suggestion that Congress codify a misuse defense in the Copyright Act,[331] such a change is likely premature; copyright misuse is not yet a firmly established area of law, and codification could ossify the defense rather than allowing it to develop through the exercise of courts' equitable discretion as new circumstances arise.[332]

E.   *Licensing of Embedded Software*

Another major area of debate in the study related to the general practice of requiring consent to the terms of a written agreement as part of the sale of a software-enabled product, particularly how such a practice would affect the lawful use of everyday products. A number of commenters raised concerns about the use of license agreements to restrict the ability of consumers to engage in legitimate activities involving their software-enabled products. In particular, these commenters expressed concern that while copyright law may authorize certain uses of embedded software, license agreements can be used to prevent those same uses.[333] These concerns, however, are not necessarily specific to embedded software.[334]

---

[326] 81 F.3d 597, 598-99 (5th Cir. 1996).

[327] *Id.* at 598-99.

[328] *Id.* at 601.

[329] *Id.*

[330] *See, e.g., Practice Mgm't Info. Corp. v. Am. Med. Ass'n*, 121 F.3d 516, 520-21 (9th Cir. 1997).

[331] CCIA Initial Comments at 4 ("Congress should consider codifying a copyright misuse provision that creates meaningful penalties that deter the willful misuse of copyrights, including in relation to exclusive rights, anticircumvention rights, and notice and takedown.").

[332] Notably, Congress recognized the equitable doctrine of patent misuse in 1988, but also created limitations to the doctrine, including a requirement that any patent misuse defense show that the patent owner has "market power," an antitrust-related condition that is not necessarily required for a finding of copyright misuse. 35 U.S.C. § 271(d); *see also* Pub. L. No. 100-703, tit. II, § 201, 102 Stat. 4674, 4676 (1988).

[333] *See, e.g.,* Aaron Perzanowski et al. Initial Comments at 5-8 (stating that licenses may frustrate acts that are otherwise legitimate under the Copyright Act, including competition, transferability, and repair); Auto Care

A common justification for imposing restrictive contractual terms in the sale of software is that it allows software companies to efficiently engage in price differentiation among different categories of purchasers.[335] As the Seventh Circuit has noted, licensing agreements allow creators to "control arbitrage" in the software industry, for example, by preventing a purchaser who obtains a consumer discount from reselling his or her copy to a commercial entity who would not be entitled to such a discount.[336] The alternative would be to modify the product—perhaps by selling consumers versions of software with lesser functionality—or to not sell to consumers at all.[337]

Many groups representing software companies echoed these points during the Office's study. One stressed that "[t]hrough licensing, software companies are able to meet the needs of a variety of different customers—whether the general public or discrete customer groups—while also protecting themselves against misuse of their rights."[338] Another observed that "[l]icensing permits a software publisher to offer a fully functional 'academic' version of its product to students at a deeply reduced price, but the rights granted do not permit use for commercial purposes."[339] In a similar vein, that group also noted that "'OEM [original equipment manufacturer] licenses' bundle software with, or install software directly on scanners or desktop computers, and require the software to be used and distributed with that hardware," in exchange for "a deep discount as part of the OEM license terms."[340] These justifications for licensing practices, however, apply across all software.

In addition, software also is increasingly being distributed under a variety of "open-source" licenses such as the GNU General Public License ("GPL")[341] or the Apache License.[342] As one commenter observed about open-source licenses, "some rightsholders . . . have determined that fewer restrictions on their software will make that software—

Ass'n Initial Comments at 3, 6 (noting concerns that vehicles cannot be repaired and manufacturers cannot create replacement parts, due to license-related restrictions).

[334] *See* MLA Initial Comments at 2 ("[C]ommon licensing models for software are in no way limited to software for these consumer products, or even to software on its own. Similar licensing models, including non-negotiable end user licensing agreements (EULAs) are very commonly used for electronic books, audiovisual works, digital sheet music, and digital sound recordings to name a few.").

[335] *See ProCD, Inc. v. Zeidenberg,* 86 F.3d 1447, 1449 (7th Cir. 1996).

[336] *Id.* at 1450.

[337] *See id.* at 1449-50 (explaining that "[i]f because of high elasticity of demand in the consumer segment of the market the only way to make a profit turned out to be a price attractive to commercial users alone, then all consumers would lose out—and so would the commercial clients, who would have to pay more").

[338] Copyright Alliance Initial Comments at 9.

[339] SIIA Initial Comments at 2.

[340] *Id.*

[341] *GNU General Public License,* GNU.ORG (June 29, 2016),https://www.gnu.org/licenses/gpl-3.0.en.html.

[342] *Licenses,* APACHE SOFTWARE FOUND., http://apache.org/licenses/.

and the devices that incorporate it—more valuable," and that "[a]s much as licensing may lead us into thorny copyright questions raised by software-enabled devices, open source licensing may lead us out of them."[343] At the same time, although open-source licenses authorize a broader range of uses than proprietary licenses, they are not wholly without restrictions. For example, while the GNU GPL gives users, among other things, the "freedom to change the software to suit [their] needs,"[344] it also requires users who make those changes to share them with the public, and to distribute the modified software under the terms of the GNU GPL.[345] Thus, even distributors of open-source software rely to some degree on the ability to enforce the terms of private agreements.[346]

Although, as noted, the practice of requiring purchasers of software-enabled consumer products to agree to certain written license terms is not uniform today, it is fair to expect that it will increase in the future. Even today there are a number of software-enabled consumer products sold under a written license containing terms regarding use of the embedded software. For instance, the Copyright Office has also found such terms applied to consumer products as thermostats[347] and security cameras.[348]

Given the apparent trend, it is appropriate for the Copyright Office to assess the various issues commenters have raised relating to EULAs and other software agreements. To the extent those concerns have particular importance in the context of embedded software, the discussion below offers views on potential avenues for resolution.

1.   Relationship to State Contract Law

A number of commenters observed that "since license terms that purport to prevent a transfer of ownership are often characterized by licensors—and interpreted by courts—

---

[343] CDT Initial Comments at 7.

[344] Brett Smith, *A Quick Guide to GPLv3*, GNU.ORG (2007), https://www.gnu.org/licenses/quick-guide-gplv3.pdf.

[345] *See GNU General Public License*, GNU.ORG (June 29, 2007), https://www.gnu.org/licenses/gpl-3.0.en.html.

[346] *See Jacobsen v. Katzer*, 535 F.3d 1373, 1381-82 (Fed. Cir. 2008) ("Copyright licenses are designed to support the right to exclude; money damages alone do not support or enforce that right. The choice to exact consideration in the form of compliance with the open source requirements of disclosure and explanation of changes, rather than as a dollar-denominated fee, is entitled to no less legal recognition.").

[347] *End User License Agreement*, NEST, https://nest.com/legal/eula/; *Smart Si Thermostat User Manual*, ECOBEE, https://www.ecobee.com/wp-content/uploads/2014/05/ecobeeSmartSi_User_Manual.pdf.

[348] *See, e.g., Myfox Final User License Contract (FULC) for Hardware, Applications and Integrated Software*, MYFOX (Apr. 5, 2016), https://www.getmyfox.com/us_en/end-user-licence-agreement.html; *End User License Agreement*, CANARY (May 19, 2016), https://canary.is/legal/eula/; *see also* MLA Initial Comments at 3 (observing, outside the context of embedded software, that "non-negotiable end user licensing agreements (EULAs) are very commonly used for electronic books, audiovisual works, digital sheet music, and digital sound recordings").

as contracts, the intersection of copyright and contract law is a necessary consideration."[349]

As these commenters appear to acknowledge, agreements accompanying the sale of software-enabled consumer products can exist regardless of copyright law. Such agreements can be understood as "ordinary contracts accompanying the sale of products . . . governed by the common law of contracts and the Uniform Commercial Code."[350] And violations of the terms of those agreements typically would constitute breach of contract, regardless of whether those violations also constituted copyright infringement.

Thus, any concerns about EULAs for embedded software cannot be fully resolved through copyright. For instance, many commenters raised concerns about license restrictions preventing consumers from freely repairing their products[351] or using interoperable products.[352] As discussed below, any *copyright* concerns regarding such activities can be resolved (as appropriate) through application of the existing copyright law—*i.e.*, a proper understanding of what constitutes "ownership" of software under the Copyright Act, and proper application of existing doctrines such as fair use. But the terms of the written contract may be enforced as a matter of state contract law regardless of the resolution of those copyright issues. And it may be that such concerns about restrictive license terms can be resolved through application of established state contract law principles. For example, commenters raised concerns about whether consumers can fairly be understood to have agreed to the terms of software licensing agreements, given their length and complexity, and the fact that they are generally "shrinkwrap" or "clickwrap" agreements.[353] Courts appear to have addressed these concerns, however, by applying standard state-law requirements for contract formation.[354] Courts also have

---

[349] *See, e.g.*, Aaron Perzanowski et al. Initial Comments at 10; *see also* CDT Initial Comments at 7; Copyright Alliance Initial Comments at 15 ("It is therefore essential that copyright law not be changed to upset basic tenets of freedom of contract.").

[350] *ProCD, Inc.*, 86 F.3d at 1450; *see also, e.g.*, *Hill v. Gateway 2000*, 105 F.3d 1147, 1149 (7th Cir. 1997) ("*ProCD* did not depend on the fact that the seller characterized the transaction as a license rather than as a contract; we treated it as a contract for the sale of goods and reserved the question whether for other purposes a 'license' characterization might be preferable."); *Moore v. Microsoft Corp.*, 293 A.D.2d 587, 587 (N.Y. 2d Dep't 2002) (enforcing the EULA under state contract law).

[351] *See* Aaron Perzanowski et al. Initial Comments at 9.

[352] *See* Public Knowledge/OTI Initial Comments at 11-12.

[353] *See, e.g.*, Tr. at 82:08-84:03 (Kit Walsh, EFF) (May 24, 2016) (noting that consumers rarely read such agreements).

[354] *See, e.g.*, *Specht v. Netscape Commc'ns Corp.*, 306 F.3d 17, 32 (2d Cir. 2002) (holding that "where consumers are urged to download free software at the immediate click of a button, a reference to the existence of license terms on a submerged screen is not sufficient to place consumers on inquiry or constructive notice of those terms"); *cf. Sgouros v. TransUnion Corp.*, 817 F.3d 1029, 1036 (7th Cir. 2016) (declining to enforce a clickwrap agreement on website where it failed to provide "reasonable notice that his use of the site or click on a button constitutes assent to an agreement"); *Nguyen v. Barnes & Noble, Inc.*, 763 F.3d 1171, 1178-79 (9th Cir.

addressed questions of unconscionability of contractual terms in software license agreements.[355]

Some commenters also suggested that state contract law might be preempted to the extent "copyright licenses reach beyond the conventional bounds of copyright (including foreclosing established limitations and exceptions such as first sale)."[356] The Copyright Office briefly addressed this issue in its *DMCA Section 104 Report* in 2001.[357] The Office noted that "copyright has long coexisted with contract law, providing a background of default provisions against which parties are generally free to order their own commercial dealings to suit their needs and the realities of the marketplace."[358] At the same time, the Office expressed concern "that right holders [sic], and not the copyright policies established by Congress, will determine the landscape of consumer privileges in the future."[359] Ultimately, the Office noted that "the issue of preemption of contractual provisions is outside the scope of the Report," but suggested that the issue "may be worthy of further consideration at some point in the future."[360] In the ensuing years, courts have continued to grapple with these issues, although the majority of them have declined to preempt state contract law with respect to such license agreements, even when these agreements touch on issues under the Copyright Act.[361]

The question of when preemption would be appropriate is a complex one that implicates *all* software licenses—and, indeed, any sort of contractual arrangement limiting the use of copyrighted works—not simply those related to embedded software.[362] As such, as in 2001, the Office believes this narrowly focused study is not the proper place to address

---

2014) (holding that there was a lack of constructive notice of a "browsewrap" agreement where the website "provide[d] no notice to users nor prompt[ed] them to take any affirmative action to demonstrate assent").

[355] *See, e.g., M.A. Mortenson Co. v. Timberline Software Corp.*, 998 P.2d 305 (Wash. 2000) (addressing unconscionability of shrinkwrap software license under state law); *cf. Comb v. PayPal, Inc.*, 218 F. Supp. 2d 1165, 1177 (N.D. Cal. 2002) (declining to enforce arbitration clause in user agreement for online service, on unconscionability grounds); *see also ProCD, Inc.*, 86 F.3d at 1449 ("Shrinkwrap licenses are enforceable unless their terms are objectionable on grounds applicable to contracts in general (for example, if they violate a rule of positive law, or if they are unconscionable).").

[356] CCIA Initial Comments at 5; *see also* Owners' Rights Initiative Initial Comments at 10-13.

[357] *See* DMCA SECTION 104 REPORT 162-64.

[358] *Id.* at 164.

[359] *Id.*

[360] *Id.* at 163-64.

[361] *Compare Vault Corp. v. Quaid Software Ltd.*, 847 F.2d 255, 268-70 (5th Cir. 1988) (preempting state contract law), *with Davidson & Assoc. v. Jung*, 422 F.3d 630 (8th Cir. 2005) (finding license agreements not preempted and thus enforceable under state contract law), *Bowers v. Baystate Techs., Inc.*, 320 F.3d 1317 (Fed. Cir. 2003) (same), *and ProCD, Inc.*, 86 F.3d at 1453-55 (same).

[362] *See, e.g.,* MLA Initial Comments at 2.

these broader questions of preemption. Ultimately, this is a matter best left to the courts to address on a case-by-case basis, applying standard preemption analysis.[363]

2. Breach of Contract versus Copyright Infringement

A related issue in this study is whether, and in what circumstances, violations of the terms of software licenses would constitute copyright infringement, as opposed to a mere breach of contract. For example, a group of law professors urged that "license agreements imposing restrictions on the use of a device or its embedded software should be enforced not with copyright remedies, but with contractual ones—subject to internal contract law limitations and copyright preemption."[364] This issue is particularly important in the context of software-enabled consumer products, given the significance of issues regarding resale, repair, tinkering, and interoperability of such products, discussed above.

This issue has been addressed by the courts repeatedly outside the context of software-enabled consumer products.[365] A leading case is the Ninth Circuit's decision in *MDY Industries, LLC v. Blizzard Entertainment, Inc.*, in which the court assessed whether the breach of a EULA and terms of use for a popular online role-playing game constituted copyright infringement.[366] The court began its analysis with the fundamental point that "[a] copyright owner who grants a nonexclusive, limited license ordinarily waives the right to sue licensees for copyright infringement, and it may sue only for breach of contract."[367] At the same time, the court acknowledged that "if the licensee acts *outside the scope of the license*, the licensor may sue for copyright infringement."[368] The court thus distinguished between "conditions," which it described as "contractual terms that limit a

---

[363] Aside from the express preemption provision in section 301, courts can assess whether enforcement of an agreement would "stand[] as an obstacle to the accomplishment and execution of the full purposes and objectives of Congress." *Hines v. Davidowitz*, 312 U.S. 52, 67 (1941); *see also Williamson v. Mazda Motor of Am., Inc.*, 562 U.S. 323, 330 (2011). For instance, while rejecting an argument that state law enforcement of a shrinkwrap software license was preempted by the Copyright Act, the court in *ProCD* "refrain[ed] from adopting a rule that anything with the label 'contract' is necessarily outside the preemption clause" of the Copyright Act, because "the variations and possibilities are too numerous to foresee." *ProCD, Inc.*, 86 F.3d at 1455. Indeed, that court expressly noted the "possibility that some applications of the law of contract could interfere with the attainment of national objectives" under the Copyright Act. *Id.*

[364] Aaron Perzanowski et al. Initial Comments at 10-11; *see also* Static Control at 3 ("Agreements with end users are not bad per se, but both parties to the agreement must know and understand the terms to which they are agreeing. Breaches of these agreements should be enforceable in contract law only, not patent or copyright law.").

[365] *See, e.g., Jacobsen*, 535 F.3d at 1380-81; *Sun Microsystems, Inc. v. Microsoft Corp.*, 188 F.3d 1115, 1121 (9th Cir. 1999).

[366] *See MDY Indus., LLC*, 629 F.3d at 939-41.

[367] *Id.* at 939.

[368] *Id.* (emphasis added).

license's scope," and "covenants," which are "all other license terms."[369] Breaches of conditions constitute copyright infringement, if the "licensee's action (1) exceeds the license's scope (2) in a manner that implicates one of the licensor's exclusive statutory rights."[370] Breaches of covenants, in contrast, are actionable only under state contract law. The *MDY* court explained that, in a given case, one must "distinguish between conditions and covenants according to state contract law, to the extent consistent with federal copyright law and policy."[371]

Another important question in this area is whether activities that Congress has expressly deemed to be "not an infringement" under the Copyright Act—such as fair use,[372] or copying or adaptation permitted under section 117[373]—can be made subject to infringement liability through private contract.[374] For instance, some EULAs for software-enabled consumer products prohibit modification or reverse engineering.[375] If a security researcher violates these restrictions in a manner that would otherwise constitute fair use, is the licensor limited to breach of contract remedies? Or can the licensor also sue for copyright infringement, even though Congress has expressly deemed that activity to be noninfringing?[376]

On the one hand, there may be an argument that private contracts should not be able to render infringing as a matter of copyright law those activities that Congress, in the Copyright Act, has determined to be noninfringing as a matter of law; it may be that the

---

[369] *Id.*

[370] *Id.* at 940.

[371] *Id.* at 939.

[372] *See* 17 U.S.C. § 107 ("[T]he fair use of a copyrighted work . . . is not an infringement of copyright.").

[373] *See id.* § 117 (providing that "[n]otwithstanding the provisions of section 106, it is not an infringement for the owner of a copy of a computer program to make or authorize the making of another copy or adaptation of that computer program" under specified circumstances).

[374] As one roundtable participant explained the issue:

> [O]ne of the most harmful practices that emerges is companies essentially writing their own law of copyright infringement . . . in a private contract[.] [O]ne means of doing this is saying you're waiving defenses to copyright infringement. You're waiving your right to reverse engineer. You're waiving your right to circumvent lawfully, to prepare lawful derivative works. . . . [N]ot all of the courts have gotten it right in saying we should treat that just as a contractual violation[.]

Tr. at 76:16-77:02 (May 24, 2016) (Kit Walsh, EFF).

[375] *See, e.g., End User License Agreement,* NEST, https://nest.com/legal/eula/ ("You agree not to . . . modify, make derivative works of, disassemble, reverse compile or reverse engineer any part of the Product Software (except to the extent applicable laws specifically prohibit such restriction for interoperability purposes . . .).").

[376] *See, e.g., Sega Enters. Ltd.,* 977 F.2d at 1520 ("Where there is good reason for studying or examining the unprotected aspects of a copyrighted computer program, disassembly for purposes of such study or examination constitutes a fair use.").

violation of such a private agreement would be actionable, at most, as a breach of contract. Allowing form agreements that are not subject to individual negotiation to extend copyright liability to activities that would otherwise be noninfringing could disrupt carefully balanced legislative policy choices, including about what kinds of activities should trigger potentially large statutory damages or attorney's fee awards.[377] On the other hand, there may be an argument that the breach of any material term of a license renders the license a nullity, such that subsequent use of the work could be infringing.[378] This is not an issue that appears to have been directly addressed in litigation,[379] and it raises complex issues that extend beyond the scope of the present study.

3. Confusion Among Consumers Regarding Licensing Terms

Another common theme raised by commenters regarding the practice of software licensing involves a consumer's lack of understanding of the terms of EULAs, and the use of complex and opaque EULAs to frustrate reasonable consumer expectations. For example, one public advocacy organization observed that "[e]ach product comes with thousands of words of legal text," and that it is *impossible* for the typical purchaser to read all of the contracts of adhesion attached to modern products and services."[380] A copyright owner organization noted in response that "[t]here is nothing specifically problematic or different about agreements for embedded software . . . than any other

---

[377] *Cf. MDY Indus., LLC*, 629 F.3d at 941 (concluding that allowing a software copyright holder to use a license to "designate any disfavored conduct during software use as copyright infringement . . . would allow software copyright owners far greater rights than Congress has generally conferred on copyright owners"); Tr. at 78:01-05 (May 18, 2016) (Keith Kupferschmid, Copyright Alliance) (suggesting—in response to a hypothetical violation of a contract that barred reverse engineering—that if a court found that activity to be fair use, it would be difficult to support an infringement claim).

[378] *See* 3 NIMMER ON COPYRIGHT § 10.15[A][2] (Matthew Bender rev. ed. 2015) (noting circumstances where "by reason of the breach of covenant, the grantor has the power to recapture the rights granted so that any further use of the work by the grantee is without authority and, hence, infringing"); 1 PAUL GOLDSTEIN, GOLDSTEIN ON COPYRIGHT § 5.3.5.1 (3d ed. Supp. 2011) (noting that in some cases a contract "obligation will be economically so material to the contract relationship that a court will treat it as a condition even though its breach does not of itself entail infringement of a right").

[379] One roundtable participant referred to the Eighth Circuit's decision in *Davidson & Assoc. v. Jung*, 422 F.3d 630 (8th Cir. 2005), as a case addressing this issue. *See* Tr. at 77:10-22 (May 24, 2016) (Kit Walsh, EFF). The Copyright Office, however, reads that case instead to have addressed the different question of whether a contractual provision prohibiting a party from engaging in certain noninfringing activities was preempted by the Copyright Act, and thus unenforceable through *contract* law. *Davidson*, 422 F.3d at 638-39. There was no claim of copyright infringement before the court of appeals, as that claim was settled at an earlier stage of the litigation. *Id.* at 637.

[380] EFF Initial Comments at 5.

type of agreement," noting that many other services impose similarly long agreements, and that such agreements "are simply a necessity of functioning in everyday society."[381]

Indeed, this is a topic arising in areas well beyond the software-enabled consumer products that are the focus of this study. In January 2016, the Department of Commerce's Internet Policy Task Force issued a White Paper addressing these issues in the context of all digital goods, including software, books, and music.[382] In examining the application of the first sale doctrine to such goods, the Internet Policy Task Force noted that online services "often" employ EULAs that "set[] forth what rights the consumer will enjoy with respect to the work, including whether he owns the copy that is transmitted and what he may do with it."[383]

The Internet Policy Task Force highlighted concerns about consumer confusion regarding the terms of the EULAs, observing that "commenters and participants on all sides agreed that consumers are entitled to clarity and that more should be done to communicate what rights they are or are not getting when they enter into a transaction involving digital transmissions of copies."[384] It concluded that "consumers would benefit from more information on the nature of the transactions they enter into, including whether they are paying for access to content or for ownership of a copy, in order to instill greater confidence and enhance participation in the online marketplace."[385] Accordingly, the Task Force recommended "the creation of a multistakeholder process to establish best practices in communications to consumers in connection with online transactions involving creative works," including "on how to inform consumers clearly and succinctly about the terms of EULAs regarding whether they 'own' the copies provided and what they may do with them."[386]

Like the Internet Policy Task Force, the Copyright Office agrees that it would be beneficial if manufacturers, as part of the sale of software-enabled consumer products, made clear what rights consumers had in the goods they were buying, including the right to resell, repair, and improve the device. As one commenter in this study noted, "rightsholders should ensure that any license that restricts the copying or use of

---

[381] Copyright Alliance Reply Comments at 5-6 ("Software licenses are no more complex or lengthy than any other agreement that consumers routinely encounter in their everyday activities. Conducting a simple Google search? That involves reading their 2,000-word agreement. Buying something on Amazon? The agreement is 3,500 words long. Purchasing a ticket on United Airlines? That agreement is about 40,000 words and close to 50 pages long."); *see also* INTERNET POLICY TASK FORCE WHITE PAPER at 68 ("This situation is hardly unique to content delivery services; consumers encounter lengthy EULAs in a wide variety of activities.").

[382] INTERNET POLICY TASK FORCE WHITE PAPER at 55-58, 68-69.

[383] *Id.* at 55.

[384] *Id.* at 57.

[385] *Id.* at 68.

[386] *Id.* at 69.

software embedded on a device is prominent to the user and that its terms are easily understood."[387] To that end, the Office believes that the multistakeholder process recommended by the Internet Policy Task Force might be productively leveraged to establish best practices for EULAs in the context of software-enabled consumer products.

V. Conclusion

The development of software embedded in everyday products is unique and promising, and has helped usher in an era in which consumers have products offering new functionality and convenience. Although these uses of software are new, that software benefits from the same existing rights and limitations as all software. This use of software does raise new issues, but the Copyright Office believes that the existing, flexible structure of the Copyright Act will serve well the needs of both copyright owners and users of software embedded in everyday products. For that reason, the Office does not recommend any legislative changes at this time. Nevertheless, the Office will continue to monitor the technological and legal landscape for further developments to ensure that copyright law moves forward and continues to promote the progress of science as envisioned in the Constitution.

---

[387] CDT Initial Comments at 7.

SUPPLEMENTARY INFORMATION: Written comments and suggestions from the public and affected agencies concerning the proposed collection of information are encouraged. Your comments should address one or more of the following four points:

—Evaluate whether the proposed collection of information is necessary for the proper performance of the functions of the agency, including whether the information will have practical utility;
—Evaluate the accuracy of the agency's estimate of the burden of the proposed collection of information, including the validity of the methodology and assumptions used;
—Enhance the quality, utility, and clarity of the information to be collected; and
—Minimize the burden of the collection of information on those who are to respond, including through the use of appropriate automated, electronic, mechanical, or other technological collection techniques or other forms of information technology, *e.g.,* permitting electronic submission of responses.

Overview of This Information Collection

(1) *Type of Information Collection:* Revision to Currently Approved Collection.

(2) *Title of the Form/Collection:* Annual Progress Report for STOP Violence Against Women Formula Grant Program.

(3) *Agency form number, if any, and the applicable component of the Department of Justice sponsoring the collection:* Form Number: 1122–0003. U.S. Department of Justice, Office on Violence Against Women.

(4) *Affected public who will be asked or required to respond, as well as a brief abstract:* The affected public includes

the 56 STOP state administrators (from 50 states, the District of Columbia and five territories and commonwealths (Guam, Puerto Rico, American Samoa, Virgin Islands, Northern Mariana Islands)) and their subgrantees. The STOP Violence Against Women Formula Grants Program was authorized through the Violence Against Women Act of 1994 (VAWA) and reauthorized and amended in 2000, 2005, and 2013. Its purpose is to promote a coordinated, multi-disciplinary approach to improving the criminal justice system's response to violence against women. The STOP Formula Grants Program envisions a partnership among law enforcement, prosecution, courts, and victim advocacy organizations to enhance victim safety and hold

offenders accountable for their crimes of violence against women. OVW administers the STOP Formula Grants Program. The grant funds must be distributed by STOP state administrators to subgrantees according to a statutory formula (as amended).

(5) *An estimate of the total number of respondents and the amount of time estimated for an average respondent to respond/reply:* It is estimated that it will take the 56 respondents (STOP administrators) approximately one hour to complete an annual progress report. It is estimated that it will take approximately one hour for roughly 2500 subgrantees [1] to complete the relevant portion of the annual progress report. The Annual Progress Report for the STOP Formula Grants Program is divided into sections that pertain to the different types of activities that subgrantees may engage in and the different types of subgrantees that receive funds, *i.e.* law enforcement agencies, prosecutors' offices, courts, victim services agencies, etc.

(6) *An estimate of the total public burden (in hours) associated with the collection:* The total annual hour burden to complete the annual progress report is 2,556 hours.

If additional information is required contact: Jerri Murray, Department Clearance Officer, United States Department of Justice, Justice Management Division, Policy and Planning Staff, Two Constitution Square, 145 N Street NE., Room 3E.405B, Washington, DC 20530.

Dated: December 9, 2015.

Jerri Murray,

Department Clearance Officer for PRA, U.S. Department of Justice.

[FR Doc. 2015–31468 Filed 12–14–15; 8 45 am]

BILLING CODE 4410–FX–P

LIBRARY OF CONGRESS

U.S. Copyright Office

[Docket No. 2015–6]

Software-Enabled Consumer Products Study: Notice and Request for Public Comment

AGENCY: U.S. Copyright Office, Library of Congress.

ACTION: Notice of inquiry.

SUMMARY: The U.S. Copyright Office is undertaking a study at the request of Congress to review the role of copyright

law with respect to software-enabled consumer products. The topics of public inquiry include whether the application of copyright law to software in everyday products enables or frustrates innovation and creativity in the design, distribution and legitimate uses of new products and innovative services. The Office also is seeking information as to whether legitimate interests or business models for copyright owners and users could be improved or undermined by changes to the copyright law in this area. This is a highly specific study not intended to examine or address more general questions about software and copyright protection.

DATES: Written comments must be received no later than February 16, 2016 at 11:59 p.m. Eastern Time. Written reply comments must be received no later than March 18, 2016 at 11:59 p.m. Eastern Time. The Office will be announcing one or more public meetings, to take place after written comments are received, by separate notice in the future.

ADDRESSES: All comments must be submitted electronically. Specific instructions for submitting comments will be posted on the Copyright Office Web site at *http://www.copyright.gov/policy/software* on or before February 1, 2016. To meet accessibility standards, all comments must be provided in a single file not to exceed six megabytes (MB) in one of the following formats: Portable Document File (PDF) format containing searchable, accessible text (not an image); Microsoft Word; WordPerfect; Rich Text Format (RTF); or ASCII text file format (not a scanned document). Both the web form and face of the uploaded comments must include the name of the submitter and any organization the submitter represents.

The Office will post all comments publicly in the form that they are received. If electronic submission of comments is not feasible, please contact the Office using the contact information below for special instructions.

FOR FURTHER INFORMATION CONTACT: Sarang V. Damle, Deputy General Counsel, *sdam@loc.gov;* Catherine Rowland, Senior Advisor to the Register of Copyrights, *crowland@loc.gov;* or Erik Bertin, Deputy Director of Registration Policy and Practice, *ebertin@loc.gov.* Each can be reached by telephone at (202) 707–8350.

SUPPLEMENTARY INFORMATION: Copyrighted software can be found in a wide range of everyday consumer products—from cars, to refrigerators, to cellphones, to thermostats, and more. Consumers have benefited greatly from this development: Software brings new

[1] Each year the number of STOP subgrantees changes. The number 2,500 is based on the number of reports that OVW has received in the past from STOP subgrantees.

qualities to ordinary products, making them safer, more efficient, and easier to use. At the same time, software's ubiquity raises significant policy issues across a broad range of subjects, including privacy, cybersecurity, and intellectual property rights. These include questions about the impact of existing copyright law on innovation and consumer uses of everyday products and innovative services that rely on such products. In light of these concerns, Senators Charles E. Grassley and Patrick Leahy (the Chairman and Ranking Member, respectively, of the Senate Committee on the Judiciary) have asked the U.S. Copyright Office to "undertake a comprehensive review of the role of copyright in the complex set of relationships at the heart" of the issues raised by the spread of software in everyday products.[1] The Senators called on the Office to seek public input from "interested industry stakeholders, consumer advocacy groups, and relevant federal agencies," and make appropriate recommendations for legislative or other changes.[2] The report must be completed no later than December 15, 2016.[3]

This study is not the proper forum for issues arising under section 1201 of the Copyright Act, which addresses the circumvention of technological protection measures on copyrighted works. Earlier this year, the Register of Copyrights testified that certain aspects of the section 1201 anticircumvention provisions of the Digital Millennium Copyright Act ("DMCA") were unanticipated when enacted almost twenty years ago, and would benefit from further review. These issues include, for example, the application of anticircumvention rules to everyday products, as well as their impact on encryption research and security testing. If you wish to submit comments about section 1201, please do so through the forthcoming section 1201 study, information on which will be available shortly at *www.copyright.gov*.

I. Background

Copyright law has expressly protected computer programs,[4] whether used in general purpose computers or embedded in everyday consumer products, since the enactment of the 1976 Copyright Act ("1976 Act"). Though the 1976 Act did not expressly list computer programs as copyrightable subject matter, the Act's legislative history makes it evident that Congress intended for them to be protected by copyright law as literary works.[5] At the same time, in the 1976 Act, Congress recognized that "the area of computer uses of copyrighted works" was a "major area [where] the problems are not sufficiently developed for a definitive legislative solution."[6] Accordingly, as originally enacted, 17 U.S.C. 117 "preserve[d] the status quo" as it existed in 1976 with respect to computer uses,[7] by providing that copyright owners had no "greater and lesser rights with respect to the use of the work in conjunction with automatic systems capable of storing, processing, retrieving, or transferring information, or in conjunction with any similar device, machine, or process, than those afforded to works under the law" as it existed prior to the effective date of the 1976 Act.[8]

Since the 1976 Act's enactment, the scope of copyright protection for computer programs has continued to be refined by Congress through legislation and by the courts through litigation. At least some of that attention has focused on the precise problem presented here: The presence of software in everyday products.

A. CONTU Report

In the mid-1970s, Congress created the National Commission on New Technological Uses of Copyrighted Works ("CONTU") to study and report on the complex issues raised by extending copyright protection to computer programs.[9] In its 1978 Report, CONTU recommended that Congress continue to protect computer programs under copyright law, specifically by amending section 101 of the 1976 Act to include a definition of computer programs and by replacing section 117 as enacted in the 1976 Act with a new provision providing express limitations on the exclusive rights of reproduction and adaptation of computer programs under certain conditions.[10] Congress adopted CONTU's legislative recommendations in 1980.[11]

While CONTU did not specifically anticipate that software would become embedded in everyday products, CONTU did recognize some general issues resulting from the fact that computer programs need a machine to operate. Specifically, CONTU recognized that the process by which a machine operates a computer program necessitates the making of a copy of the program and that adaptations are sometimes necessary to make a program interoperable with the machine.[12] CONTU preliminarily addressed these issues by including in its recommended revisions to section 117 a provision permitting the reproduction or adaptation of a computer program when created as an essential step in using the program in conjunction with a machine, finding that "[b]ecause the placement of a work into a computer is the preparation of a copy, the law should provide that persons in rightful possession of copies of programs be able to use them freely without fear of exposure to copyright liability."[13] CONTU's recommendations for the new section 117 also included a provision permitting the making of copies and adaptations for archival purposes.[14]

At the same time, CONTU foresaw that the issues surrounding copyright protection for software would have to be examined again by Congress and the Copyright Office:

[T]he Commission recognizes that the dynamics of computer science promise changes in the creation and use of authors' writings that cannot be predicted with any certainty. The effects of these changes should have the attention of Congress and its appropriate agencies to ensure that those who are the responsible policy makers maintain an awareness of the changing impact of computer technology on both the needs of authors and the role of authors in the information age. To that end, the Commission recommends that Congress, through the appropriate committees, and the Copyright Office, in the course of its administration of copyright registrations and other activities, continuously monitor the impact of computer applications on the creation of works of authorship.[15]

B. Computer Software Rental Amendments Act of 1990

A decade later, in response to concerns that commercial rental of

[1] Letter from Sen. Charles E. Grassley, Chairman, Senate Committee on the Judiciary, and Sen. Patrick Leahy, Ranking Member, Senate Committee on the Judiciary, to Maria A. Pallante, Register of Copyrights, U.S. Copyright Office, at 1 (Oct. 22, 2015), *available at http //www copyright gov/ policy/software*

[2] *Id* at 2.

[3] *Id*

[4] Although the Copyright Act uses the term "computer program," *see* 17 U.S.C. 101 (definition of "computer program"), the terms "software" and "computer program" are used interchangeably in this notice.

[5] *See* H.R. Rep. No. 94–1476, at 55 (1976); *see also* National Commission on New Technological Uses of Copyrighted Works, Final Report of the National Commission on New Technological Uses of Copyrighted Works 16 (1978) ("CONTU Report").

[6] H.R. Rep. No. 94–1476, at 55.

[7] *Id*

[8] Public Law 94–553, sec. 117, 90 Stat. 2541, 2565 (1976).

[9] *See* CONTU Report at 3–4.

[10] *Id* at 12.

[11] *See* Act of Dec. 12, 1980, Public Law 96–517, sec. 10, 94 Stat. 3015, 3028–29.

[12] *See* CONTU Report at 12–14.

[13] *Id* at 12–13.

[14] *Id.*

[15] *Id* at 46.

computer programs would encourage illegal copying of such programs, Congress passed the Computer Software Rental Amendments Act of 1990 (''Computer Software Rental Act''), which amended section 109 of the Copyright Act to prohibit the rental, lease or lending of a computer program for direct or indirect commercial gain unless authorized by the copyright owner of the program.[16] Notably, Congress also expressly provided an exception to this prohibition for ''a computer program which is embodied in a machine or product and which cannot be copied during the ordinary operation or use of the machine or product.''[17] In doing so, Congress recognized that computer programs can be embedded in machines or products and tailored the rental legislation to avoid interference with the ordinary use of such products.[18]

C. DMCA

Congress revisited the issues surrounding software and copyright law with the DMCA.[19] As particularly relevant here, the DMCA amended section 117 of the Copyright Act to permit the reproduction of computer programs for the purposes of machine maintenance or repair following a court of appeals decision[20] that cast doubt on the ability of independent service organizations to repair computer hardware.[21] This provision foreshadows the more general concerns raised by the spread of software in everyday products—namely, that maintaining or repairing a software-enabled product often will require copying of the software. Section 104 of the DMCA also directed the Office to study the effects of the DMCA amendments and the development of electronic commerce

and associated technology on the

operation of sections 109 and 117 of the Copyright Act, as well as ''the relationship between existing and

emergent technology and the operation of sections 109 and 117.''[22] The Office subsequently published a report detailing its findings and recommendations in August 2001 (''Section 104 Report'').[23]

The Section 104 Report discussed a number of issues relevant to the discussion of software in everyday products. For instance, it addressed proposals to add a ''digital first sale'' right to section 109 of the Copyright Act to explicitly grant consumers the authority to resell works in digital format. Although the Office concluded that no legislative changes to section 109 were necessary at the time, it recognized that ''[t]he time may come when Congress may wish to consider further how to address these concerns.''[24] In particular, the Office anticipated some of the issues presented here when it highlighted ''the operation of the first sale doctrine in the context of works tethered to a particular device''—an example of which would be software embedded in everyday products—as an issue worthy of continued monitoring.[25] Additionally, the Office noted the concern that unilateral contractual provisions could be used to limit consumers' ability to invoke exceptions and limitations in copyright law. Although the Office concluded that those issues were outside the scope of the study, and that ''market forces may well prevent right holders from unreasonably limiting consumer privileges,'' it also recognized that ''it is possible that at some point in the future a case could be made for statutory change.''[26]

D. Developments in Case Law

In the meantime, courts, too, have

weighed in on a number of issues

concerning copyright protection of software, including copyrightability, the application of the fair use doctrine, and ownership of software by consumers. In analyzing these issues, however, courts have not generally distinguished between software installed on general purpose computers and that embedded in everyday products.

Courts have helped define the scope of copyright protection for software and address questions of infringement through application of doctrines such as the idea/expression dichotomy (codified in 17 U.S.C. 102(b)), merger, and *scè nes*

à *faire*.[27] The idea/expression dichotomy, as applied to software, excludes from copyright protection the abstract ''methodology or processes adopted by the programmer'' in creating the code.[28] In the context of software, the merger doctrine excludes certain otherwise creative expression from copyright protection when it is the only way, or one of a limited number of ways, to perform a given computing task.[29] The *scè nes à faire* doctrine has been used to limit or eliminate copyright protection for elements of a program that are dictated by external factors or by efficiency concerns, such as the mechanical specifications of the computer on which the program runs.[30]

The fair use doctrine, codified in 17 U.S.C. 107, is also relevant here. Courts have applied the fair use doctrine to permit uses of software that ensure interoperability of software with new products and devices. For example, in *Sega Enterprises Ltd.* v. *Accolade, Inc.,* the Court of Appeals for the Ninth Circuit held that copying a video game console's computer program to decompile and reverse engineer the object code to make it interoperable with video games created by the defendant was a fair use.[31] Similarly, in *Sony Computer Entertainment, Inc.* v. *Connectix Corp.,* the court held that reverse engineering the operating system of a PlayStation gaming console to develop a computer program allowing users to play PlayStation video games on a desktop computer, as well as making copies in the course of such reverse engineering, was a fair use.[32]

Another important issue courts have tackled involves the scope of section 117's limitations on exclusive rights in computer programs. Section 117(a) allows copies or adaptations of

[16] *See* Public Law 101–650, 104 Stat. 5089, 5134–35 (1990); 17 U.S.C. 109(b)(1)(A).

[17] 17 U.S.C. 109(b)(1)(B)(i).

[18] *See Computer Software Rental Amendments Act (H R 2740, H R 5297, and S 198) Hearing Before the Subcomm on Courts, Intellectual Prop , and the Admin of Justice of the H Comm on the Judiciary,* 101st Cong. 15–16 (1990) (statement of Rep. Mike Synar) (''Some parties have interpreted the [Computer Software Rental Act] as potentially affecting computer programs which may be contained as a component of another machine, such as a program which drives a mechanized robot or runs a microwave or a household kitchen utensil. Such a result was not intended and will be addressed in this legislation.'').

[19] Public Law 105–304, 112 Stat. 2860 (1998).

[20] *MAI Sys Corp* v. *Peak Computer,* 991 F.2d 511 (9th Cir. 1993).

[21] *See* DMCA, sec. 302, 112 Stat. 2860, 2887 (1998); S. Rep. No. 105–190, at 21–22 (1998).

[22] DMCA, sec. 104, 112 Stat. 2860, 2876 (1998).

[23] *See generally* U.S. Copyright Office, DMCA Section 104 Report (2001).

[24] *Id* at 96–97.

[25] *Id* at xvi–xvii.

[26] *Id* at 162–64.

[27] *See, e g , Lexmark International, Inc* v. *Static Control Components, Inc ,* 387 F.3d 522, 534–36 (6th Cir. 2004); *Apple Computer, Inc* v. *Franklin Computer Corp ,* 714 F.2d 1240, 1252–53 (3d Cir. 1983); *Computer Management Assistance Co* v. *DeCastro,* 220 F.3d 396, 400–02 (5th Cir. 2000).

[28] H.R. Rep. No. 94–1476, at 9; *see also* CONTU Report at 22 (''[C]opyright leads to the result that anyone is free to make a computer carry out any unpatented process, but not to misappropriate another's writing to do so.'').

[29] *See* CONTU Report at 20 (''[C]opyrighted language may be copied without infringing when there is but a limited number of ways to express a given idea. . . . In the computer context, this means that when specific instructions, even though previously copyrighted, are the only and essential means of accomplishing a given task, their later use by another will not amount to an infringement.'').

[30] *See, e g , Lexmark,* 387 F.3d at 535–36 (outlining applicability of doctrine to computer programs).

[31] 977 F.2d 1510, 1527–28 (9th Cir. 1992), *amended by* 1993 U.S. App. LEXIS 78 (9th Cir. 1993).

[32] 203 F.3d 596, 602–08 (9th Cir. 2000).

computer programs to be made either ''as an essential step in the utilization of the computer program in conjunction with a machine'' or for archival purposes, but this provision may only be invoked by ''the owner of a copy of a computer program.'' [33] This raises difficult questions regarding whether a consumer owns a copy of software installed on a device or machine for purposes of section 117 when formal title is lacking or a license purports to impose restrictions on the use of the computer program. Courts have provided somewhat conflicting guidance regarding this issue, and the application of the law can be unclear in many contexts.[34]

E. Recent Legislation

Issues associated with the spread of copyrighted software in everyday products have prompted legislative action in an attempt to address some of the copyright issues created by the spread of such works.[35] In the context of section 1201—which, as explained, is the subject of a separate Copyright Office study—Congress enacted legislation in August 2014 to broaden the regulatory exemption permitting the circumvention of technological measures for the purpose of connecting wireless telephone handsets to wireless communication networks (a process commonly known as ''cellphone unlocking'').[36]

The Unlocking Technology Act of 2015, as most pertinent to this study, would amend section 117 of the Copyright Act to permit the reproduction or adaptation of ''the software or firmware of a user-

purchased mobile communications device for the sole purpose of . . . connect[ing] to a wireless communications network'' if the reproduction or adaptation is initiated by or with the consent of the owner of the device, the owner is in legal possession of the device, and the owner has the consent of the authorized operator of the wireless communications network to use the network.[37] The legislation would also limit the prohibition on circumvention in section 1201 of title 17 to circumstances where circumvention is carried out in order to infringe or facilitate the infringement of a copyrighted work, and would permit the use of or trafficking in circumvention devices unless the intent of such use or trafficking is to infringe or facilitate infringement.[38]

In addition, the You Own Devices Act (''YODA'') would amend section 109 of the Copyright Act to allow the transfer of ownership of a copy of a computer program embedded on a machine or other product ''if [the] computer program enables any part of [that] machine or other product to operate,'' as well as any right to receive software updates or security patches from the manufacturer.[39] This right of transfer could not be waived by any contractual agreement.[40] In addition, the original owner of the device would be prohibited from retaining an unauthorized copy of the computer program after transferring the device and the computer program to another person.[41]

F. Relationship to Questions About Section 1201

Some issues related to software embedded in everyday products have come to the forefront in recent years through the 1201 rulemaking process. As the Copyright Office has frequently noted, the 1201 rulemaking can serve as a barometer for larger public policy questions, including issues that may merit or would require legislative change. The public should not submit concerns about section 1201 through this software study, but rather through the Copyright Office's forthcoming study on section 1201, information about which will be available shortly at *http://www.copyright.gov/.*

II. Subjects of Inquiry

In response to the letter from Senators Grassley and Leahy, the Office is seeking public comment on the following five topics. A party choosing to respond to this Notice of Inquiry need not address every subject, but the Office requests that responding parties clearly identify and separately address each subject for which a response is submitted.

1. The provisions of the copyright law that are implicated by the ubiquity of copyrighted software in everyday products;

2. Whether, and to what extent, the design, distribution, and legitimate uses of products are being enabled and/or frustrated by the application of existing copyright law to software in everyday products;

3. Whether, and to what extent, innovative services are being enabled and/or frustrated by the application of existing copyright law to software in everyday products;

4. Whether, and to what extent, legitimate interests or business models for copyright owners and users could be undermined or improved by changes to the copyright law in this area; and

5. Key issues in how the copyright law intersects with other areas of law in establishing how products that rely on software to function can be lawfully used.

When addressing these topics, respondents should consider the following specific issues:

1. Whether copyright law should distinguish between software embedded in ''everyday products'' and other types of software, and, if so, how such a distinction might be drawn in an administrable manner.

a. Whether ''everyday products'' can be distinguished from other products that contain software, such as general purpose computers—essentially how to define ''everyday products.''

b. If distinguishing between software embedded in ''everyday products'' and other types of software is impracticable, whether there are alternative ways the Office can distinguish between categories of software.

2. The rationale and proper scope of copyright protection for software embedded in everyday products, including the extent to which copyright infringement is a concern with respect to such software.

3. The need to enable interoperability with software-embedded devices, including specific examples of ways in which the law frustrates or enables such interoperability.

4. Whether current limitations on and exceptions to copyright protection

[33] 17 U.S.C. 117(a).

[34] *Compare Krause* v. *Titleserv, Inc*, 402 F.3d 119, 124 (2d Cir. 2005), *with Vernor* v. *Autodesk, Inc*, 621 F.3d 1102, 1111 (9th Cir. 2010).

[35] Bills have also been introduced addressing related issues outside copyright law stemming from the spread of software in everyday products. The Spy Car Act of 2015 would direct the National Highway Traffic Safety Administration to conduct a rulemaking and issue motor vehicle cybersecurity regulations protecting against unauthorized access to electronic systems in vehicles or driving data, such as information about a vehicle's location, speed or owner, collected by such electronic systems. SPY Car Act of 2015, S. 1806, 114th Cong. sec. 2 (2015). A discussion draft introduced in the Commerce, Manufacturing, and Trade Subcommittee of the Energy & Commerce Committee of the House of Representatives would prohibit access to electronic control units or critical systems in a motor vehicle. A Bill to provide greater transparency, accountability, and safety authority to the National Highway Traffic Safety Administration, and for other purposes [Discussion Draft], 114th Cong. sec. 302 (2015), *available at http //docs house gov/meetings/IF/IF17/20151021/ 104070/BILLS-114pih- DiscussionDrafton VehicleandRoadwaySafety pdf*

[36] *See* Unlocking Consumer Choice and Wireless Competition Act, Public Law 113–144, 128 Stat. 1751 (2014).

[37] Unlocking Technology Act, H.R. 1587, 114th Cong. sec. 3 (2015).

[38] *Id* sec. 2.

[39] YODA, H.R. 862, 114th Cong. sec. 2 (2015).

[40] *Id.*

[41] *Id.*

adequately address issues concerning software embedded in everyday products, or whether amendments or clarifications would be useful. Specific areas of interest include:

a. The idea/expression dichotomy

(codified in 17 U.S.C. 102(b))

b. The merger doctrine

c. The *scènes à faire* doctrine

d. Fair use (codified in 17 U.S.C. 107)

e. The first-sale doctrine (codified in 17 U.S.C. 109)

f. Statutory limitations on exclusive rights in computer programs (codified in 17 U.S.C. 117)

5. The state of contract law *vis-à-vis* software embedded in everyday products, and how contracts such as end user license agreements impact investment in and the dissemination and use of everyday products, including whether any legislative action in this area is needed.

6. Any additional relevant issues not raised above.

Dated: December 9, 2015.

Maria A. Pallante,

Register of Copyrights, U.S. Copyright Office.

[FR Doc. 2015–31411 Filed 12–14–15; 8 45 am]

BILLING CODE 1410–30–P

NATIONAL ARCHIVES AND RECORDS ADMINISTRATION

Information Security Oversight Office

[NARA–2016–007]

State, Local, Tribal, and Private Sector Policy Advisory Committee (SLTPS–PAC) Meeting

AGENCY: National Archives and Records Administration (NARA).

ACTION: Notice of Advisory Committee Meeting.

SUMMARY: In accordance with the Federal Advisory Committee Act (5 U.S.C. app 2) and implementing regulation 41 CFR 101–6, NARA announces the following committee meeting.

DATES: The meeting will be on January 27, 2016, from 10:00 a m. to 12:00 p.m. EDT.

ADDRESSES: National Archives and Records Administration; 700 Pennsylvania Avenue NW.; Jefferson Room; Washington, DC 20408.

FOR FURTHER INFORMATION CONTACT: Robert J. Skwirot, Senior Program Analyst, by mail at ISOO, National Archives Building; 700 Pennsylvania Avenue NW ; Washington DC 20408 by

SUPPLEMENTARY INFORMATION: The purpose of this meeting is to discuss matters relating to the Classified National Security Information Program for State, Local, Tribal, and Private Sector Entities. The meeting will be

open to the public. However, due to space limitations and access procedures,

you must submit the name and telephone number of individuals planning to attend to the Information Security Oversight Office (ISOO) no later than Friday, January 22, 2016. ISOO will provide additional instructions for accessing the meeting's location.

Dated: December 8, 2015.

Patrice Little Murray,

Committee Management Officer.

[FR Doc. 2015–31526 Filed 12–14–15; 8 45 am]

BILLING CODE 7515–01–P

NATIONAL LABOR RELATIONS BOARD

Notice of Appointments of Individuals To Serve as Members of Performance Review Boards; Correction

Authority: 5 U.S.C. 4314(c)(4).

AGENCY: National Labor Relations Board.

ACTION: Notice; correction.

SUMMARY: The National Labor Relations Board published a document in the **Federal Register** of November 25, 2015, giving notice that certain named individuals had been appointed to serve as members of performance review boards in the National Labor Relations Board for the rating year beginning

October 1, 2014 and ending September telephone number at (202) 357–5398, or by email at *robert.skwirot@nara.gov*. Contact ISOO at *ISOO@nara.gov*.

By Direction of the Board.

William B. Cowen,

Solicitor.

[FR Doc. 2015–31421 Filed 12–14–15; 8 45 am]

BILLING CODE 7545–01–P

NUCLEAR REGULATORY COMMISSION

[Docket Nos. 50–275, 50–323, and 72–26; NRC–2015–0244]

Pacific Gas and Electric Company; Diablo Canyon Power Plant, Units 1 and 2, and Diablo Canyon Independent Spent Fuel Storage Installation

AGENCY: Nuclear Regulatory Commission.

ACTION: Finding of no significant impact with associated environmental

assessment; final issuance.

SUMMARY: The U.S. Nuclear Regulatory Commission (NRC) is issuing an environmental assessment (EA) and finding of no significant impact (FONSI) related to a request to amend the Facility Operating License Nos. DPR–80, DPR–82, and SNM–2511 issued to Pacific Gas and Electric Company (PG&E), for operation of the Diablo Canyon Power Plant, Units 1 and 2, including the specific-license Independent Spent Fuel Storage

Installation (hereinafter DCPP or the

facility), located in San Luis Obispo County, California. The requested amendments would permit licensee security personnel to use certain firearms and ammunition feeding devices not previously permitted, notwithstanding State, local, and certain Federal firearms laws or regulations that otherwise prohibit such actions.

30, 2015. The document failed to list one of the individuals so appointed.

FOR FURTHER INFORMATION CONTACT: Gary Shinners, Executive Secretary, National Labor Relations Board, 1099 14th Street NW., Washington, DC 20570, (202) 273–3737 (this is not a toll-free number), 1–866–315–6572 (TTY/TDD).

Correction

In the **Federal Register** of November 25, 2015, in FR Doc. 2015–30031, on page 73836, in the third column, correct the list of names of individuals appointed to serve as members of performance review boards by adding the following individual:

Name and Title

Deborah Yaffee—Director, Office of Appeals

Dated: December 9, 2015.

ADDRESSES: Please refer to Docket ID NRC–2015–0244 when contacting the NRC about the availability of information regarding this document. You may obtain publicly-available information related to this document using any of the following methods:

• Federal Rulemaking Web site: Go to *http://www.regulations.gov* and search for Docket ID NRC–2015–0244. Address questions about NRC dockets to Carol Gallagher; telephone: 301–415–3463; email: *Carol.Gallagher@nrc.gov.* For technical questions, contact the individual listed in the **FOR FURTHER INFORMATION CONTACT** section of this document.

• NRC's Agencywide Documents Access and Management System (ADAMS): You may obtain publicly-available documents online in the ADAMS Public Documents collection at

estimated for an average respondent to respond: Of the approximately 18,000 government law enforcement agencies that are eligible to submit cases, it is estimated that thirty to fifty percent will actually submit cases to ViCAP. The time burden of the respondents is less than 60 minutes per form.

6. *An estimate of the total public burden (in hours) associated with the collection:* 5,000 annual burden hours.

If additional information is required contact: Jerri Murray, Department Clearance Officer, United States Department of Justice, Justice Management Division, Policy and Planning Staff, Two Constitution Square, 145 N Street NE., 3E.405B, Washington, DC 20530.

Dated: March 23, 2016.

Jerri Murray,
Department Clearance Officer for PRA, U.S. Department of Justice.
[FR Doc. 2016–06900 Filed 3–25–16; 8 45 am]
BILLING CODE 4410–02–P

LIBRARY OF CONGRESS

Copyright Office

[Docket Nos. 2015–6, 2015–8]

Software-Enabled Consumer Products Study and Section 1201 Study: Announcement of Public Roundtables

AGENCY: U.S. Copyright Office, Library of Congress.
ACTION: Notice of public roundtables.

SUMMARY: The United States Copyright Office has issued Notices of Inquiry (''NOIs'') announcing separate public studies on software-enabled consumer products and section 1201 of title 17. In addition to soliciting written comments on these issues, the Office is now announcing public roundtables for these studies to provide forums for interested members of the public to address the issues set forth in the NOIs.

DATES AND ADDRESSES: Public roundtables for the above-referenced Copyright Office studies will be held on the dates and at the locations provided below. The roundtables for the two studies are being held on consecutive dates in each location to accommodate parties who may have an interest in attending both.

Software-Enabled Consumer Products Study: For its study on software-enabled consumer products, the Office will hold public roundtables in Washington, DC and San Francisco, CA. The roundtable in Washington will take place on May 18, 2016, at the Library of Congress's Madison Building, 101 Independence

Avenue SE., Washington, DC 20540, from 9:00 a m. to approximately 5:00 p.m. The roundtable in San Francisco will take place on May 24, 2016, at Hastings School of Law, 200 McAllister Street, San Francisco, CA 94102, from 9:00 a m. to approximately 5:00 p.m.

Section 1201 Study: Likewise, for its study on section 1201, the Office will hold public roundtables in Washington, DC and San Francisco, CA. The roundtable in Washington will take place on May 19 and May 20, 2016, at the Library of Congress's Madison Building, 101 Independence Avenue SE., Washington, DC 20540, from 9:00 a m. to approximately 5:00 p.m. on the first day, and from 9:00 a.m. to approximately 1:00 p m. on the second day. The roundtable in San Francisco will take place on May 25 and May 26, 2016, at Hastings School of Law, 200 McAllister Street, San Francisco, CA 94102, from 9:00 a m. to approximately 5:00 p.m. on the first day, and from 9:00 a m. to approximately 1:00 p.m. on the second day.

Additional information, including instructions for submitting requests to participate in the roundtables, is available on the Copyright Office Web site at *http://copyright.gov/policy/software/* (software-enabled consumer products) and *http://copyright.gov/policy/1201/* (section 1201). Requests to participate in the roundtables must be received by the Copyright Office by April 18, 2016. If you are unable to access a computer or the internet, please contact the Office using the contact information below for special instructions.

FOR FURTHER INFORMATION CONTACT:
Software-Enabled Consumer Products Study: Sarang V. Damle, Deputy General Counsel, *sdam@loc.gov;* Catherine Rowland, Senior Advisor to the Register of Copyrights, *crowland@loc.gov;* or Erik Bertin, Deputy Director of Registration Policy and Practice, *ebertin@loc.gov.*

Section 1201 Study: Regan A. Smith, Associate General Counsel, *resm@loc.gov;* or Kevin Amer, Senior Counsel for Policy and International Affairs, *kamer@loc.gov.*

Each of these persons can be reached by telephone at (202) 707–8350.

SUPPLEMENTARY INFORMATION: The Copyright Office is conducting separate studies concerning software-enabled consumer products and section 1201 of title 17.

Software-Enabled Consumer Products Study

On December 15, 2015, the Copyright Office issued an NOI announcing a study on the role of copyright law with

respect to the design, distribution, and use of consumer products that include embedded software. 80 FR 77668. This study is being done at the request of the United States Senate Committee on the Judiciary. Consistent with the Committee's request, the focus of the study is on software contained in consumer products; it is not intended to address more general questions about software and copyright.

Section 1201 Study

Enacted in 1998 as part of the Digital Millennium Copyright Act (''DMCA''), section 1201 prohibits the circumvention of technological measures employed by or on behalf of copyright owners to control access to their works (also known as ''access controls''), as well as the trafficking in technologies or services that facilitate such circumvention. In addition, section 1201 codifies a triennial rulemaking process through which the Librarian of Congress, upon the recommendation of the Register of Copyrights, can grant exemptions to the prohibition on the circumvention of access controls. The Copyright Office issued an NOI soliciting comments on the operation and effectiveness of section 1201 on December 29, 2015. 80 FR 81369.

Roundtable Subjects of Inquiry

At this time, the Copyright Office is providing notice of its intention to seek further input for these studies through public roundtables to be held on the dates and at the addresses set forth above. The public roundtables will offer an opportunity for interested parties to comment on topics set forth in the NOIs.

For the software-enabled consumer products study, the roundtables at each location will consist of sessions on the following topics: (1) The proper role of copyright in protecting software-enabled consumer products; (2) ownership and contractual issues; (3) fair use; and (4) the first sale doctrine, section 117, and other limitations and exceptions. After the final session, the Office will also provide participants and observers with an opportunity to offer additional comments for the record.

For the section 1201 study, roundtables at each location will consist of sessions on the following topics: (1) The relationship of section 1201 to copyright infringement, consumer issues, and competition; (2) the rulemaking process—evidentiary and procedural issues; (3) the rulemaking process—renewal of previously granted exemptions; (4) the anti-trafficking prohibitions and third-party assistance for permitted circumvention of technological measures; and (5) permanent exemptions to the prohibition on circumvention. After the final session, the Office will also provide participants and observers with an opportunity to offer additional comments for the record.

Each of the roundtable hearing rooms will have a limited number of seats for participants and observers. Public seating for observers will be provided on a first-come, first-served basis on the days of the roundtables.

Dated: March 23, 2016.

Maria A. Pallante,

Register of Copyrights, U.S. Copyright Office.

[FR Doc. 2016–06925 Filed 3–25–16; 8 45 am]

BILLING CODE 1410-30-P

LIBRARY OF CONGRESS

Copyright Royalty Board

[Docket No. 2008–2 CRB CD 2000–2003 (Phase II)]

Distribution of the 2000, 2001, 2002 and 2003 Cable Royalty Funds

AGENCY: Copyright Royalty Board, Library of Congress.

ACTION: Final distribution order.

SUMMARY: The Copyright Royalty Judges announce the final Phase II distribution of cable royalty funds for the years 2000, 2001, 2002 and 2003 for the Program Suppliers programming category.

DATES: Effective March 28, 2016.

ADDRESSES: The final distribution order also is posted on the Copyright Royalty Board Web site at *http://www.loc.gov/crb.*

FOR FURTHER INFORMATION CONTACT: Kimberly Whittle, Attorney Advisor. Telephone: (202) 707–7658; Email: *crb@loc.gov.*

SUPPLEMENTARY INFORMATION: The captioned consolidated royalty distribution proceeding concluded on August 14, 2015, when the United States Court of Appeals for the DC Circuit issued a mandate relating to

their June 30, 2015, order affirming the distribution shares for claimants in the

Program Suppliers category as determined by the Copyright Royalty Judges (Judges). After the mandate, the Judges received filings from Worldwide Subsidy Group dba Independent Producers Group (IPG) and the Motion Picture Association of America (MPAA) contesting the appropriate methodology for distribution of the remaining royalty funds on deposit.

By order dated November 25, 2015, the Judges directed MPAA to provide historical context from which the Judges and the Licensing Division of the

Copyright Office could distribute accurately the funds, taking into account prior partial distributions, fund growth through accrued interest, and deductions for Licensing Division costs. MPAA provided the necessary information on December 7, 2015. The Licensing Division staff provided accounting services to assure accurate distribution in accordance with the Judges' orders.

The Licensing Division calculated that, as of February 17, 2016, the total distribution to IPG for each royalty year should be:

2000	$617,719
2001	164,203
2002	197,725
2003	125,884
Total	1,105,531

Now, therefore, the Judges hereby *order* that the Licensing Division make final distribution to IPG from the Program Suppliers category for the years 2000 through 2003, inclusive, in the amounts listed, adjusted if necessary to reflect interest accrued or costs incurred from and after February 17, 2016, to the date of distribution.

The Judges *further order* that the Licensing Division distribute simultaneously the remaining funds in the Program Suppliers category for royalty years 2000 through 2003, inclusive, to MPAA, adjusted if necessary to reflect interest accrued or costs incurred from and after February 17, 2016.

The Judges *further order* that IPG and MPAA provide to the Licensing Division all necessary and pertinent information to facilitate the transfer by March 31, 2016.

Dated: March 23, 2016.

Suzanne M. Barnett,

Chief Copyright Royalty Judge.

[FR Doc. 2016–06923 Filed 3–25–16; 8 45 am]

BILLING CODE 1410-72-P

www.ingramcontent.com/pod-product-compliance
Lightning Source LLC
Chambersburg PA
CBHW081210180526
45170CB00006B/2281